POSITIVE POWER

Your Path to a Higher Leadership Profile

James L. Fisher

Executive
Excellence
Publishing

For permission requests, contact the publisher at:

Executive Excellence Publishing
1366 East 1120 South
Provo, UT 84606
Phone: 1-801-375-4060
Toll Free: 1-800-304-9782
Fax: 1-801-377-5960
www.eep.com

For Executive Excellence books, magazines and other products, contact Executive Excellence directly. Call 1-800-304-9782, fax 1-801-377-5960, or visit our website at www.eep.com.

Printed in the United States

Printed by Publishers Press

10 9 8 7 6 5 4 3 2 1

Library of Congress Cataloging-in-Publication Data

Fisher, James Lee, 1931-
  Positive power : your path to a higher leadership profile / James Lee Fisher.
    p. cm.
Includes index.
  ISBN 1-930771-24-X
  1. Leadership. 2. Management. I. Title.
  HD57.7 .F577 2001
  658.4'092--dc21
                        2001004518

To my mother, Vera Brant Fisher;
my father, Morris L. Fisher; and my children,
Kerry, Kathy, Curtis and John.

"This landmark book is a remarkable combination of intelligence and practicality. Rich in substance, insight and counsel, it establishes an indisputable and unique foundation and from there it is applied to every dimension of personal and professional life in the workplace."
—Harold Chappelear, former President and COO, Medicis Pharmaceutical Corporation

"As *Power of the Presidency* was the single most important book ever written about the college presidency, *Positive Power* will light the way for all who would lead in any arena."
—Dr. Charles Smith, former Chancellor, University of Tennessee Board of Regents

"In this provocative book, Jim Fisher challenges leaders to embrace rather than fear power. Each chapter presents remarkable suggestions, both grand and modest, by which executives can learn to exercise the power necessary for effective leadership."
—Dr. Rita Bornstein, President, Rollins College

"Jim Fisher realizes that power can be used equally for good or for evil. The purpose of this book is to empower us to do good."
—Rev. Theodore M. Hesburgh, C.S.C., President Emeritus, University of Notre Dame

"As a close observer of Dr. Fisher for over 35 years, I have witnessed his appetite for engaging increasingly complex undertakings. Not only did his approach create a record of admirable successes but acted also as a catalyst that enhanced the careers of those who followed his approach. This book clearly presents a proven methodology to those who have a drive to be creative and useful."
—Homer B. Martin, MD, Psychiatric Consultant to Healthcare Review Corporation

"Having bridged the military and higher education, *Positive Power* is universal, often amazing, always instructive, and completely unique. A product of Jim Fisher's rich experience and insight coupled with his most extraordinary reading of the significant research on leadership and power. His applications will completely inspire and enable readers regardless of their initial scores on the Fisher Leadership Profile included in the book."

—Rear Admiral Richard I. Ridenour, M.D. (Ret), President, Marian College of Fond du Lac, Wisconsin

"This is the first book on leadership I have ever really understood. It gets to the point. If you want to make it, read it."

—Tom Koch, Chairman, Curtis Engine, Inc.

"A singular achievement, completely original in its wisdom as it is applied to every aspect of personal and professional life in a corporate world."

—Burnell Kraft, former Senior Vice President, Archer Daniels Midland Company

"After the first 10 pages, I couldn't put it down. As soon as I finished it, I gave it to my corporate executive son."

—David Richardson, retired grain merchant and former Marine

"This is the book we have been waiting for Jim Fisher to write, a comprehensive book on leadership."

—Dr. Vance Peterson, President, Council for the Advancement and Support of Education (CASE)

"One of the most interesting and helpful management books I've read to date."

—Edward DelGiorno, Chair of the Board, Hood College and Senior Vice President, First Data Corporation

So long as a man's power is bound to the goal, the work, the calling, it is, in itself, neither good nor evil, only a suitable or unsuitable instrument. But as soon as this bond with the goal is broken off or loosened, and the man ceases to think of power as the capacity to do something, but thinks of it as a possession, then his power...is evil...

—Buber

Henry IV, Part I

The skipping king, he ambled up and down
With shallow jesters and rash bavin wits...
Mingled his royalty with capering fools,
Had his great name profaned with their scorns...
Grew a companion to the common streets,
Enfeoff'd himself to popularity;
That, being daily swallowed by men's eyes,
They surfeited with honey and began
To loathe the taste of sweet-ness, whereof a little
More than a little is by much too much.
So when he had occasion to be seen,
He was but as the cuckoo is in June,
Heard, not regarded; seen, but with such eyes
As, sick and blunted with community,
Afford no extraordinary gaze,
Such as is bent on sun-like majesty
When it shines seldom in admiring eyes; ...
Being of his presence glutted, gorged, and full.

Table of Contents

Preface

The idea for this book first developed as I was writing *Power of the Presidency*. That book was written for college and university presidents, and was reviewed generously as "the best ever written" on the subject. Since that time I have written several others, but always with this more generic book in mind. During this period each of my four children took positions in some kind of corporation, both profit and non-profit. Occasionally, they asked me questions, and we often discussed problems that came up in their work. All of them, I thought, were talented and ambitious and could, if they chose, go up the corporate ladder.

Nonetheless, I continued writing academic papers and books on leadership in colleges and universities. Time passed and *Power of the Presidency* went into its fourth printing. Reviewers wrote of its generic applications. I was invited to lecture on campuses and before professional groups. At the same time, a spate of interesting books hit the popular market which implied, and later even spoke of a new, stronger style of leadership. Major newspapers and trade and professional journals featured countless articles on the subject. I started writing this book. As much as I appreciated the other efforts, I wanted to write a completely different one—a book that would be fundamentally substantive, broader in scope, complete, and more directly related to the individual as a force for organizational influence. Virtually all the other books and articles neglected or glossed over the primary condition of leadership—power; and the few that discussed power did so from incomplete or misleading assumptions. And virtually none were sufficiently personal to be of any real value to would-be rising executives in corporations. This book explores these dimensions. Its intent is to insure success and reasonable happiness.

Acknowledgements

This book is the result of countless hours of dialogue with intelligent and candid people. I continue in your debt: Rita Bornstein of Rollins College; Gene Budig of baseball's American League, Harold Chappelear of The Upjohn Company and Medicis Pharmaceutical Corporation; Ed DelGiorno of First Data Corporation; George Dragas of The Dragas Companies; Bruce Heilman of the University of Richmond; Rev. Theodore M. Hesburgh of the University of Notre Dame; Jim Koch of Old Dominion University; Tom Koch, Curtis Engine, Inc.; Burnell Kraft of Archer Daniels Midland Company; Homer Martin, M.D., of Healthcare Review Corporation; LtCol P. Neal Meier, USMC (Ret.); Scott Miller of Wesley College; Zell Miller, United States Senate; James Murray of the American Council on Education; Mark Perkins of Towson University; Vance Peterson of Council for the Advancement and Support of Education (CASE); George Pruitt, Thomas Edison State College; David Richardson, a high school buddy and former Marine; Rear Admiral Richard I. Ridenour (Ret.); MajGen Wayne Rollings, USMC (Ret.); Kenneth "Buzz" Shaw, Syracuse University; Charles Smith of the University of Tennessee; and Tim and Carolyn Thyreen of Waynesburg College.

I thank Nathan Lyon and Courtney Hammond for their excellent editing, and I am deeply indebted to Sheryl Tucker who typed and retyped so many manuscripts that she knows the book by heart.

Introduction

Power is the essence of leadership. Power is the ability to influence others. Power enables one to act effectively, to persuade, to lead so as to achieve a significant action. Power is the ability of A to persuade B to do something B might otherwise not do. Power moves others to do what otherwise would go undone. Power in its purest sense is as ethical or unethical as action. Power is leadership.

If you choose the road to power, you need not be apologetic. Your life will never want for excitement, opportunity, or fun. Combined with personal goodness, power is a worthy life force because it is exhilarating and presses you to completely engage life. When put to a worthy cause, what a life it can be! When beleaguered, you may wish for greater peace or anonymity, and for more "close personal relationships." But if you use power right, you will have a full measure of these things and be able to rest in the knowledge that yours has been a full and worthwhile life.

To use power to accomplish worthwhile purposes is the most moral life of all. Do not avoid the arena because of the sanctimoniousness of those less certain. Do not accept the ugly connotations of the word that makes others uncomfortable and eventually deceitful as they covertly engage in life's normal power plays. Our every word and gestures are attempts to influence, to engage in the shallow waters of power. Why not go in further, to the deeper, more varied, challenging and rewarding waters where the real action is? If this appeals to you as an individual, I hope this book serves as a helpful guide. Let us proceed carefully, thoughtfully, and with a smile.

The Essence of Power

When are men most useless, would you say? When they can't command and can't obey.

—Goethe

Power does not corrupt men; fools, however, if they get into a position of power, corrupt power.

—George Bernard Shaw

Power tends to corrupt, and absolute power corrupts absolutely.

—Lord Acton

Absolute power is okay, if you're careful.

—Julius Caesar

This book is intended to help you achieve extraordinary success and reasonable happiness in both your work and your personal life. It is based on replicable research, experience and a deep appreciation of history. I do not presume this is a definitive statement, but it is a blend of research, personal observation and experience into a candid and understandable guide for individual behavior in a professional setting. It may also prove valuable in other areas of your life. I ask only that you read it carefully, think about it seriously, and finally accept or reject its suggestions as you make your own choices. While I have tried to blend in humor, the ideas are offered thoughtfully.

Although you are understandably impatient to get to the action of this book, that is—"What should I do, or consider doing in order to be more powerful, influential, successful, loveable, and happy?"—understanding a subject is absolutely essential to its mastery. You can become a virtuoso on the instrument of power.

Read these first four chapters carefully before going into the more direct suggestions in the following sections. I suggest rereading them before going on because the concepts discussed are immutable and can be applied in any role, professional or personal. If you thoroughly understand them, you will think of many other ways to apply them personally that I haven't anticipated.

St. Simone

The key to having personal power and success is the extent to which you can maintain proper distance in most of the meaningful relationships in life. I shall discuss this factor in a variety of ways throughout this book.

Keep in mind this allegory about a man named Simone that relates to effective distancing. Simone, an early Christian ascetic, felt the need to dramatically demonstrate to others that the then popular and easy Church was not the essence of the faith. To do so, Simone erected a 60-foot tower topped by a platform. For 20 years he stayed up there, preaching to the multitudes who came to observe the spectacle. When the rains and storms would come, he laced his body to the platform to keep from being blown off. The ropes would eat into his flesh leaving open wounds. Afterwards, maggots would feed from his wounds. Should one fall from his place, Simone would reach down and return it to his flesh saying, "Eat what God has given you." Simone was so effective from the platform the Roman Catholic Church made him a saint. When he came down after 20 years he was asked what was the most difficult part of those years. St. Simone replied, "Getting on top of the platform."

So it is with effective leaders. The most difficult aspect of their position is not the climb

> Ronald Reagan, an actor and former sports announcer who was no gifted student, never left his platform and was considered "the great communicator."

up to and securing the appointment, but getting onto the executive platform and staying firmly put. The elevated platform was Simone's way of projecting an aura of distance and mystery about his person, a medium which gave his message the most impact. Other mediums include: the pulpit, the state, the throne, the limousine, the right dress, or the blue suit. You should also choose your medium, only in a more subtle and less dramatic way than Simone. This is called *social distance*.

Exercising power well and often appears to observers as a magical and God-given talent. It is mysterious, but not God-given. And it is the

> ### The Importance of Social Distance
>
> President Jimmy Carter, a good and intelligent man, compromised social distance from the first day when he eschewed the limousine and decided to walk down Pennsylvania Avenue. Later, he admitted "lustful" thoughts to *Playboy* magazine. When he appeared in a television ad for a second term in a sweater and open collar at 2:00 am, most Americans thought he should have been in bed. He lost the election.

key to effective leadership. Others give power willingly to those who manifest qualities and traits that elicit a supportive response. Quite naturally, those who aren't successful rationalize their failures by saying the successes of others are of little value. Or that others have been favored in special and unwarranted ways.

When perplexed and in difficulty, those who can learn from failure (and most don't) review their own unsuccessful approach and compare it with those who succeed. What are their special characteristics? Why do some succeed and others fail in both work and in personal relationships?

How much you know about power can be fundamentally valuable to you in life and work. The replicable literature of power can be accepted or rejected. But all who are intelligent, thoughtful, and at all ambitious should at least study it. In this way, insights can be achieved that serve well throughout life and instill inspiration, meaning, and success into what was before a largely uncertain and even vacuous experience. Rarely does one intuitively grasp the basic principles of power and leadership, but they can be learned and used by virtually anyone who is highly motivated and reasonably intelligent.

Power Is Basic in All of Us

Power is a basic ingredient of the individual psyche and, therefore, to society. Virtually all psychologists, sociologists, political scientists, and historians agree that the ability to influence or control is one of the vital drives of human life. Leaders in any setting are simply people more adept in using power than others. Everyone tries to influence others, whether in work, love, or play.

Surely no thoughtful observer of human behavior can deny that much of human life is a ceaseless search for identity, recognition, and importance. It is a search starting at birth when the infant realizes that personal welfare usually varies with the esteem others hold for them. This never changes. This process invariably leads to attempts to either submit to or exert influence (power) over others. Psychologists have long recognized power as a central concept in any attempt to understand social behavior. People are usually more comfortable with the euphemistic term "influence." I use the words interchangeably because power may wear different cloaks—influence, persuasion, leadership, control, love, friendship, faith—depending on specific situations and style of the individual.

Most human expressions are designed to influence or to impress others. Think about it. This is true on the job, in politics, with friends and loved ones, in a religious or social group, or during a cocktail conversation or a poker game. It is true of nearly all interactions. The extent to which you successfully influence another is directly proportional to your positive self-esteem.

Success enhances self-esteem further. So, each experience can be a learning process and reinforce self-worth. Those who fail too often become frustrated, cynical, and eventually bitter. People who manage power poorly are more likely to reinforce a negative personal image again and again. Those who are unwilling to exercise reasonable power and influence will inevitably experience more conflict and unhappiness throughout their lives.

Mental health and self satisfaction are founded in the intricacies of interpersonal influence. In effect, the more resources you control, the more secure you feel. If your position is shaky, you tend to be unhappy and insecure. If you are on a course of declining power, you make the most foolish mistakes of your life. Because everyone is involved in the process of acquiring and using power, the real question boils down to the extent to which more "good" rather than "bad" guys understand and use the power process in a positive and appropriate way rather than in a negative, destructive, and inappropriate way.

Contrary to what many think, a good leader is not one who seeks personal success, is gregarious and seeks affiliation, or speaks of personal problems. A good leader is one who savors the interplay of power and its impact, and who is not the "buddy" or the colleague. Uncomfortable as it may seem to some, power is a reality of organizational (and personal) life and all relationships, however casual. And the effective use of power is critical in all organizations that would be productive and contributing. The same is true for individuals within the organization.

> ### Losing Power and Your Senses
>
> In leaving office, Bill Clinton's every move seemed to be a caricature. Starting with extreme pardons involving big contributors, drug dealers, and family, this ordinarily intelligent man leased a Manhattan office at $500,000 a year and finally moved to Harlem in the wake of playing several rounds of golf at a closed Florida country club. Why did this man who had so masterfully influenced the public for more than two decades suddenly lose it?

Getting results is more important to effective persons than either the need for personal recognition or the need to be liked by others. Despite the emphasis placed on recognition and acceptance, these two characteristics most often discourage productive and effective leadership. The highly self-centered nature of the personal achiever invariably leads to disharmony in an organization. The person with a strong need to be liked is precisely the one who wants to stay on good terms with

> ### Why Wasn't Don Promoted?
>
> Five years ago, Don, a B+ business student in college, won a $60,000 per year job with Motorola. He immediately bonded with his fellow new employees. He drank beer with them and although not much of a player, never missed a departmental softball game. He shared confidences and personal matters with his new associates. In time, because he was a genuinely good guy and very sincere, he developed close friendships with many in the company.
>
> Don also worked hard, he performed effectively and was well liked. Many in his hiring group were promoted to management positions, yet five years later, good old Don was still in the same job. He wondered why.

everybody, and therefore, is the one who will make concessions when strength is needed. The need to be liked leads a person to indulge people in order to gain favor. The essential distancing for leadership is lost in this ineffective and ultimately anxious process. Camaraderie may be established but the price paid is a loss of respect and no significant change.

So, to be most effective, you must have a desire for positive impact, for being strong and influential. Moreover, this desire must take priority over the need for personal recognition or the need to be liked by others. Effectiveness naturally brings recognition and friendship.

Attitudes Toward Power Are Usually Uninformed and Often Dishonest

Many people think only shady and devious characters engage in acts of power. As I have said, the fact is almost all of our own subtle efforts to influence others are power acts which convey the same inevitable psychological consequences for us as for those dark, pernicious figures.

That force we call power is the most mysterious, abused, and misunderstood dynamic component of human interaction. Although it has fascinated people through the ages, experts have only recently begun to focus on power systematically and with scientific objectivity. Research on power is still rarely cited in the corporate and academic literature. This is unfortunate, but understandable. We rarely view our personal characteristics with a disinterested calm. Power is simply too uncomfortable a subject to be compatible with the philosophy implied in most writing on management, leadership and personal relationships. Until recently, most who wrote about corporate America seemed more concerned with harmony and process than with results. While TQM, re-engineering et al. attempts to combine the two, their results are expensive and increasingly questionable. Harmonious relationships in organizations are desirable in most situations; these relationships do not spring from egalitarianism and parity, but from a mix of structure and freedom inspired and empowered by strong leadership. Power and structure in an organization give rise to both harmony and production.

Because proclaimed values, theory, and practice often conflict, it is understandable to ignore topics such as power. At American colleges and universities, for instance, although studies have established that college professors quickly recognize and acknowledge power centers and individuals, few will discuss power candidly because such discussion violates comfortable beliefs about the nature of universities and academic life. But everyone knows where the power is and wants as much of it as possible.

Yet interest in power or its euphemisms seems timely and is generating even greater awareness. In airport book stores, there invariably seem to be at least two anxious coveys of people looking furtively over their shoulders to see if anyone is watching. One group huddles around books on how to be more attractive, lovable, and sexy. The second group concentrates on the books on how to be important, assertive, and successful. Truly knowing and using power will obviate both interests and more nearly ensure a balanced life.

Finally, before proceeding, we should more clearly distinguish between motives for power (although sadly, any power motive, base or altruistic, yields results). A person's desire for impact may take either of two primary forms: 1) an orientation toward achieving personal gain and aggrandizement, or 2) an orientation toward achieving gain for all or the common good.

In the first instance, the need for power is so self-serving that it is unhealthy. In the second instance, the person's motivation is more "socialized" and power (or leadership) is valued as benefitting a larger mission or goal, the results of which benefit many. This book focuses on personal motivation that includes broader benefits to more people or the common good.

There are those who hold that influencing others is more of an art than a science, more of an accident than a plan. They are mistaken, and this is to your advantage. When conducted well, continuous effective influence requires finesse and has an artistic quality, but it can only be exercised well from a base of intelligence. This is the primary premise of this book. While we may vary in our capacity to learn, virtually any motivated person can become influential through an appreciation of power, ergo a leader. Read on.

- In the spirit of St. Simone, never, never get off your platform.
- Much of life is a bluff anyway.

The Forms of Power

Man is a make-believe animal; he is never so truly himself as when he is acting a part.

—William Hazlitt

Severities should be dealt out all at once, that by their suddenness they may give less offense; benefits should be handed out drop by drop, that they may be relished the more.

—Machiavelli

Men are never attached to you by favors.

—Napoleon

Now to the rules of power, a topology that must be indelibly imprinted on your mind as you proceed. Power is the ability of A to persuade B to do something B might not otherwise do. Read this again. Say it! Leadership, a euphemism, is simply a disguise for power. Leadership without power is impossible, for power, in its various forms, is the substance of leadership. So let's fuel your mind before charting your course.

Researchers agree that the bases of power are diverse and vary in degrees from one situation to another. They also tend to agree that a combination of conscious and unconscious factors are engaged to influence others. Some years ago two scholars at the University of Michigan, French and Raven, presented a topology on power that, for the first time, granted students of leadership an objective analytical and complete approach. Virtually every definition of leadership (from transactional to transformational) fell under one of the five of the French and Raven power forms: coercion, reward, legitimate, expert, and charismatic. These are the five keys to influence, to extraordinary leadership. Their work was so remarkable that an "aha!" moment echoed across the academic spectrum. Indeed, I wrote my third book, *Power of the Presidency*, with these power forms in mind. But enough rationale, you should simply know that it exists and can be substantiated directly or indirectly by many empirical studies.

In reality, leadership and power are the same thing, that is, they both represent the ability of one person to get another to do something that he or she might otherwise not

> ### Transactional and Transformational Leadership = Power
>
> *Transactional* leadership is based on a transaction or exchange that takes place when the leader rewards, disciplines, or informs the follower depending on the performance of the follower. The *transactional* leader employs the first four power forms: coercion, reward, legitimate and expert.
> The *transformational* leader motivates others to do more than they had intended or thought possible. The *transformationalist* employs all five power forms but remarkably transcends all with the fifth, charisma. It is charisma which makes the effective leader and which all reasonably intelligent highly motivated persons can develop.

have done. Think on this: leadership is simply a synonym for power. Power is at once both broader and more specific than traditional definitions of leadership. The forms of power are more conducive to further analysis. In fact, there is less confusion about the power forms than leadership. For the purpose of understanding, inclusion and implementa-

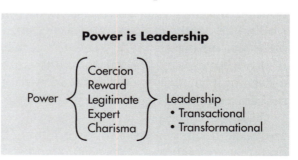

Power is Leadership

Power { Coercion, Reward, Legitimate, Expert, Charisma } Leadership
• Transactional
• Transformational

tion of leadership, one must understand the forms of power. We then will call leadership what it is, power.

These are the French and Raven power forms, from least to most effective: coercion, reward, legitimate, expert, and charismatic. Burn them into your mind.

Going Down

The transactional leader is like the guy who jumps off a 26-story building and says as he passes the 23rd floor, "Things look okay so far."
—Colonel P. Neal Meier, USMC(Ret)

Coercive Power Is the Most Used and Least Effective

Coercive power uses threats and punishments to gain compliance. Although it works, it is the least effective kind of power for a leader, yet many would-be leaders believe that it is the key to authority. You should know that the threat of punishment induces

greater conformity than punishment itself, for once punishment is actually used, it becomes increasingly less effective. We also know that the leader's perceived legitimacy reduces resistance to conformity and makes punishment more acceptable to the

Selective Coercion

During the administration of George Washington, Alexander Hamilton counseled Washington to use federal troops to put down rebellious farmers in N.Y. The new Federal Government was scarcely strong enough to quiet a serious rebellion, but it was certainly strong enough to squash a small uprising that could be used as an example for the rest of the country. It worked, the Whiskey Rebellion was put down and there were no more serious uprisings against the new Federal Government.

punished, and if the leader is generally admired, followers even more readily accept the use of penalties. For long-lasting changes in behavior, it is best to avoid the use of punishment. Early on, a leader in a new position may use punishment but only once—and used effectively, after that example, it rarely need be employed again. But if further penalties must be enacted, then do so quickly and, if possible, through a delegate.

We have also found that maturity tends to reduce the already questionable value of punishment as a motivating condition; that more mature groups tend to be more productive under less punitive conditions. However, even highly educated people are willing to administer punishment when commanded to do so by established authority figures. Studies have established this to a frightening extent. When educated individuals are ordered to administer "dangerous" degrees of electric shock or other punishing conditions to others, they almost invariably do so. Bear in mind that only less confident leaders tend to rely more heavily on coercive power than on other forms of influence. Typically, its use is a sign that your effectiveness is wavering and you should be moving on.

When other forms of power are wanting—that is, when a supervisor is not granted sufficient authority to exercise power (by a board or a boss) he or she may be more inclined to use covert and coercive means to obtain ends. Therefore, organizations that allow excessive authority to be assumed by employees will be less effective because their supervisors do not have the ability (power) to grant the privilege of participation; it is simply assumed as a right by the participants. Executives are bound to develop diminished feelings of self-worth and be less effective. This leads to a greater reliance upon the use of coercion and less effective results. Under these conditions, supervisors are often moved to use fear, arousal, and stealth as influence techniques. Clearly, as the powerholder's expectations of successful influence rise, there is an increasing tendency to exert more pressure by the use of coercive influence.

Implied Coercion

President Theodore Roosevelt's foreign policy of "Speak softly but carry a big stick" is a perfect example of the effective use of implied coercion. Roosevelt reshaped American foreign relations by a combination of charm and muscle.

In summary, although the threat of punishment or penalty tends to induce compliance, an astute leader uses it rarely. On those few occasions, the individual punished should be isolated as much as possible from community support. Making a public example of someone, however, may prove useful since the action will not remain secret long anyway. Never apply punishment in anger or pique but only after thoughtful deliberation, because you will probably abandon the idea. Time usually suggests another, wiser, and more just form of inspiration that better serves your worthy goals.

Reward Power is Debatable

Through reward power, the second least effective form of influence, an individual accomplishes desired outcomes by giving favors, recognition, or rewards to group members. Studies have revealed some very interesting examples. For instance, high status people tend to compromise the stated goals of their organization or group more readily than others: The higher the office, the more likely the leader is to compromise. Authority figures who yield too readily to their group are more likely to be exploited by the group. This suggests that the leader should maintain psychological distance from the members of the group, which we will discuss later in this chapter. Nice guys, at least to the degree that they compromise their offices, do finish last. The oft discussed idea of consensus or collegial leadership in this light is ludicrous.

Although difficult to do, it is often better to reward those we do not like or those we feel dissimilar to than those to whom we are attracted. This statement assumes that it is easier to influence those who are attractive or similar to us, and that more effort is required with dissimilar personalities. The main message is that the effective leader rewards those who support the goals of the organization, regardless of personal feeling. Rewards are also a way to bring personality opposites into the fold. Unfortunately, leaders too often use rewards to prevent rather than to eliminate existing resistance.

Rewards are not likely to change attitudes permanently. Rather, when rewards cease, the rewarded person typically reverts to former original attitudes and behavior. Furthermore, withholding rewards results in resentment. So don't expect too much from bestowing recognition, favors, or money on others. Rewards will not replace expert and charismatic power, which we will discuss later.

On the other hand, rewards do make a difference in behavior. The failure of the Soviet Union makes this point dramatically.

> Machiavelli warned the Prince that "liberality" (rewards) could not guarantee that the Prince would be held in high regard by his followers. In fact, Machiavelli concluded that it was better to be feared than to try to gain support with rewards.

Indeed, the entire field of economics is based on the premise that rewards influence behavior. You must reward those who contribute to your goals.

In relatively democratic situations, coalitions almost invariably develop and parity emerges as a social principle. Left without structure (legitimate power), contractual agreements develop and power is diffused. Participants develop feelings of identification between each other, resulting in parity without discrimination and a reduction in the effectiveness of the leader and the organization. In recent years the concept of equality over equity unfortunately gained even more acceptance. More and more people found "share and share alike" to be more acceptable than the traditional notion that rewards followed personal effort and contribution. Consequently, quality and production in corporate America (profit and non-profit) dropped to all time lows. Among equals no one can lead.

For instance, in terms of merit pay (the only effective way to pay), the astute executive, while reserving final authority, should delegate responsibility for salaries and promotion to others, directing controversy elsewhere. There will always be controversy in such matters. (In the case of collective bargaining, reward power is so diffused that it is virtually nonexistent, but this is another book.)

The higher-ranking leader should use reward power more subtly. For example, use selective words or notes of praise or make appointments to key committees. There is no substitute for thoughtful, deliberate, sincere acknowledgment and support from the leader. But positive reinforcement regarding salary and promotion is wisest. Use merit pay but, if possible, let others do it. Most importantly, bear in mind always that there are limits to the secure and effective use of reward power. While you must pay for performance, you simply cannot buy worthwhile support. So use it, but don't count on it.

Legitimate Power Is Your Platform

To be most effective, the leader needs structure, form, station, authority, and protocol; a position from which to be inspiring and charming. Legitimate power is your platform. Get on it and stay there, but wear it warmly and believe in it. You must accept the prerequisites and authority of your position and, from the first day, appear to live comfortably with them. Never apologize for or downplay your position. To do so is simply a way of telling others that you are not deserving of your office, and it guarantees that you will be less effective.

Legitimate power is based on a group's acceptance of common beliefs and practices. The acceptance of these practices and values, which include the distribution of influence within the particular setting, binds those members together through their common perspective. The group adheres to leaders who appear to fit certain roles consistent with their expectations, endowing those persons who assume leadership with certain power. For instance, a general, chairman, mother, judge, president, manager, doctor, priest, or senator all, within a given context, grant legitimate power to the individual. Certain activities and actions come to be expected and accepted from those leaders and are considered legitimate. The acceptance of common norms enables a leader to exercise power that otherwise might not be accepted by the group. *By so legitimizing power, its exercise is transformed in a remarkable way, for it makes the use of all other power forms (coercive, reward, expert, and charismatic) more acceptable to the group.* Remember this.

> ### Kimberly's Platform
>
> Kimberly was promoted from Account Executive at T. Rowe Price to a vice presidency of her division. She was happy, her fellow account executives were happy for her and had a party to celebrate her promotion.
>
> But Kimberly knew her new job called for different and changed relationships with her former colleagues. From her first day on the job, Kimberly behaved differently. She remained warm and charming, but she no longer crossed the line of either personal or professional reciprocity; she was now the boss.
>
> At her first staff meeting, she explained her new role and expectations. She told them why their relationship had to change for their mutual benefit.
>
> At first her former peers questioned and considered her calculating, but as time passed, they saw the same Kimberly in a new role, one of leadership designed to improve conditions for them. More time passed and Kimberly became the most admired and productive vice president in the company.

For instance, in most social situations, the exercise of power involves costs. We pay the cost of resources, make commitments, and have a greater need to rely on the other power forms. In effect, we use up our potential for influencing the group. Why? Because in most situations, we expect parity of opinion to prevail. In effect, without legitimate authority, we are expected to take turns on center stage. Clearly, the possession of legitimate power or authority will, if used effectively, significantly enhance the effectiveness of the leader, for it will not cost other power forms. Indeed, people in legitimate authority positions are expected to use their authority. But most newly appointed executives are afraid to exercise the limited authority they have. Their anxiety and uncertainty make them the ones who say, "Wait a while until I get the lay of the land." By the time they realize their mistakes, it's too late. This initial uncertainty has long-lasting effects on the executive's ability to assume power. Conversely, often too little authority is given to those who are expected to lead. Bosses and boards tend to limit the authority of a legitimatized figure, and then wonder why the person can't produce up to expectation. During recent years, this has happened to countless executives in industry, education, and government. Stripped of legitimate authority, it is almost impossible to lead.

People generally follow legitimate leaders with whom they agree. Those with whom they disagree are likely to be sent packing, ignored or subverted. That's the reason expert and charismatic powers are so important to you (but more on these later). While legitimate power is a significant element of influence and control, like coercive and reward power, it is not as effective as most people think. You need more than legitimacy. People who do not at least reluctantly agree with their leader will often disobey or ignore. In extreme cases, they may even try to overthrow the leader.

Power Vacuum

Eaton College, a small school in the northwest, was having problems in enrollment, and finances were increasingly precarious. The president of many years was finally retired and replaced by a new president with impressive scholarly credentials who was a collegial leader.

In what he thought was the best academic style, he made decisions by consensus. He simply would not make a decision that was not the result of labored meetings, consultation, and compromise. Although increasingly involved in every issue, the faculty and staff finally became contentious and unhappy. They petitioned the Board of Trustees to remove him from office.

Eaton then sought a new President, and this time they pointedly sought an experienced transformational leader, regardless of academic credentials.

And legitimate leaders who noticeably overstep the bounds of their roles invite needless resistance.

A common and troublesome situation arises when a delegated leader will not discharge his or her office. I term this a "power vacuum," the antithesis of a competent application of power leadership. This occurs when the appointed leader, for whatever reason, will not assume the responsibilities of the office. Assignment to a legitimate leadership role does not confer any leadership abilities, only the potential for leadership. Unfortunately, an individual may be promoted to a position of authority and then become paralyzed. Co-workers then assume, diffuse, and diminish it until there is no power force. During this period, both production and morale always drop.

Nonetheless, it is important to emphasize that within formal organizations, such as most companies and corporations, norms and expectations invariably develop that make the exercise of power expected and accepted. Thus, social control of behavior becomes an expected part of corporate life. *Legitimate power is of fundamental importance to all executives who would be leaders because once power becomes legitimized, it will not be resisted unless it is abused or ineffectively used*. Once power becomes legitimate, it no longer depends on the resources or arguments or power that produced it in the first place. It can stand alone as a form of power. Indeed, the more legitimate the leader becomes, the more the group accepts the leader, and the greater it judges his or her competence. The more legitimate the leader, the more the leader is endowed with superior personal qualities. And, the more legitimate the leader,

Learning the Hard Way

Laura, an egalitarian, became CEO of a new company, but she was the boss in name only. Indeed, she thought this was the way to go, but then the problems began. There was conflict and no one was really in charge. Her two partners had worked together before and generally supported each other at her expense. Now the company is in deep debt and will most likely be dissolved. "Today, I would not give up one ounce of power and control," she says. "I would even treat partners as employees."

the more effectively he or she can exercise the wonderful "incremental" forms of power that follow—*expert* and *charismatic* power.

Bear in mind that holding a position of high status does not automatically make you a leader, it simply gives you a great advantage in your effort. The higher you go, the more careful you must be in resisting the tendency toward detail, inflexible procedure, and a custodial mentality. These are the kinds of things behind which the unsuccessful executive hides.

Legitimate power is maintained not so much by its originating sanctions, but rather by the degree to which the group continues to adhere to the common and unifying bonds that produced the legitimate leader in the first place. If a holder of legitimate power, such as a corporate officer, a judge, a store manager, or a college president, conducts the office poorly, then power again becomes diffused. The group spends more time in conflict than in growth. Legitimate power adds stability to the group and can only be used effectively after you thoroughly understand and appreciate the other forms of power. Most companies neglect this fact completely, and this will be to your advantage.

It is also fairly well established that group members perceive an

Failed Leadership

A short while ago I was watching a merchant ship tie up in a 20-25 knot wind in Baltimore Harbor. A senior-looking officer standing on the flybridge harshly ordered a crew member to "Tighten that damn spring-line." The crew member acidly answered back "it's not my job." A younger officer on the main deck came over and demanded that the crewman tighten the spring-line. The crewman responded "I have a contract as an engineer on this ship." The junior officer said "I don't give a damn. Either tighten the spring-line or I'll knock you on your _____." The crew member tightened the spring-line.

According to the definition, "A" did finally get "B" to do something that "B" might not have otherwise gotten done, but what kind of leadership was it? Transformational or transactional? The answer? Clearly transactional. In one case, the leader tried to use legitimate power and failed; in the other, the leader used coercive power. And it worked. Both are examples of less effective forms of leadership—coercion and legitimate power, and both distinctly transactional. The senior officer attempted to use legitimate power but failed because he acted beyond the limits of his contractual relationship with the seaman. The junior officer succeeded using the threat of punishment for noncompliance regardless of the ship's contract with the seaman but he surely made a future enemy. Ultimately both officers failed.

organization's status structure more accurately when high status members react *less extensively* throughout the organization and retain final authority. That is, to be an effective leader you cannot be the "good buddy" type. This does not mean that you should not frequently move around in the company being warm and friendly, but it does mean that you should not become overly involved or intimate in your course. Indeed, legitimate power largely depends on the extent to which group members perceive the role in the first place, and they cannot perceive you as their leader if you are too involved with them. People are less inclined to be resentful and hostile when they are operating under common and understood norms with fully legitimized leaders. And, appointed leaders are generally considered more legitimate and effective than elected leaders. Rather than making a leader more secure and effective, election generally tends to result in anxiety, insecurity, and vulnerability.

One further word here: The recent documentation of the loss of public confidence in most contemporary institutions has consequences for decision making in all corporate life. The acceptance of some form of authority is critical to all forms of organizations. As we have established, it is impossible to exercise control of general direction exclusively by using rewards and punishments (although both are legitimizing power agents), nor can it be done with consistent effectiveness by using exclusively expert or charismatic power. We simply must have a legitimate power base with sufficient authority to back it up. Even anthropologists advise us that while thrones may be out of fashion, authority still requires a cultural frame in which to define itself and advance its claims.

It takes a masterful, legitimate leader to overcome the currents of general society effectively. Examples are corporate leaders under conditions of extreme unionism, religious leaders during periods of demysticism, and political and educational leaders during periods of egalitarianism. Because when everyone has a piece of the action (power), little or nothing gets done. The tyranny of the many is every bit as evil as the tyranny of the few.

The discussion of expert and charismatic power, which follows, represents a kind of "incremental power" characteristic of an individual. Legitimate, reward, and coercive power tend to be organizationally derived and are transactional instruments. That is, the legitimizing agent (corporation, country, church, society itself) enables the leader to hold position and to reward or punish, but it is the truly extraordinary person who weaves in these next two near magical forms of power. Most people of reasonable ability and motivation can exercise these first three forms of power. *But those who adroitly use charismatic and expert power from a legitimate base will be the most effective leaders.*

Expert Power Is Knowledge or the Perception of Knowledge

Expert power, which reflects the deference accorded a perceived authority, grants influence and power. Expert power in most circumstances is the most consistently effective kind of power of those discussed so far. There are two ways to wield the influence of an expert. You can be introduced to a group as an expert, and unless you commit a monumental blunder, you will be the controlling influence in the group. Or, you can actually become an expert, a person who is knowledgeable and informed about the subject at hand. The difference between the two may be obscure to observers who are inclined to accept expert power uncritically. For example, forecasts are accepted and influential in decision making even though attempts to predict the future are suspected by members of the group as being inaccurate. It is also true that appearing to withhold information or expertise is a measurably significant power form.

As a leader attempts to garner support for a particular cause, it is clearly valuable to be perceived as an expert. This reception both inspires support for a common cause and reduces unproduc-

An Expert in Disguise Is Still an Expert

Professor Davis wanted to demonstrate to his graduate business students the power of expertise, real or perceived. He invited a group of graduate art students to a seminar conducted by one Jacques DeGalle, a well known authority on French and American impressionism. The subject was the comparative quality of the two schools of art.

Now Jacques was really Jeremy Wilson, a bright young assistant professor of English, who had been asked to read a book on French and American impressionism.

At the end of four hours of intense discussion, Jacques the bogus, had more influence on the outcome than all of the graduate art students.

tive conflict. Most preferable is that the leader be a true authority on both the nature and condition of the enterprise. People frequently accept expert pronouncements because it takes time and effort for an opponent to gather information for an alternative position. Most are not willing to risk the loss of popularity that is at stake when going against the confident leader.

Research further demonstrates the value of perceived expertise. People introduced as prestigious feel better accepted and more at ease than people assigned low-prestige roles. They are measurably more effective and influential. Remember this when you introduce speakers or others you would have influence your people.

Groups with more than one expert are less certain of their judgment, and even the experts are less effective. This recognition explains the old Marine Corps adage, "It's better to have one idiot in charge than two geniuses." The more acknowledged experts in a group, the less effective their expert powers. Even the experts become inhibited. In groups with many experts, high status (legitimate power) rather than expertise can be the more significant determinant of behavior. Combining expertise with high position is a most effective posture, providing the leader demonstrates expertise consistently. Therefore, you should rarely speak in groups unless you are certain of your subject. You do not enjoy the luxury of spontaneous brilliance or foolishness.

In sum then, knowing more about the subject than others, combined with the legitimacy of an office itself, gives you a decided advantage in any situation. You should always try to be perceived as knowledgeable, which means that you will rarely participate in groups of other experts, will delegate as many details as possible, will always strive for greater expertise, and will often refrain from speaking. As leader, your main job is to inspire, occasionally offering an occasional trace of detail merely to imply your greater knowledge. If you are wrong or mistaken, admit it. But don't make mistakes too often or dwell on them unnecessarily when you do.

Charismatic (Referent) Is the Most Effective Form of Power

Charismatic power, the single most effective form of power and the ultimate in personal power, is based on the admiration and liking that people feel toward an individual. The charismatic leader has a great ability to inspire trust and confidence, to be esteemed. Some researchers have used the term "referent power" for this category, and others have used public presence, heroic or charismatic. I prefer charismatic, in spite of its sometimes uncomfortable connotations, because it is more commonly used. This is not the charisma of divine inspiration, a special gift, grace, or talent that some have and most have not, but rather a quality of trust and confidence that you can *honestly* cultivate.

For centuries, philosophers have viewed gaining the affection, trust, and respect of others as the most effective form of leadership. Throughout history and literature, we can find people who have become heroes simply by winning the adulation of others. People feel secure with these heroes; some go so far as to become worshipful. People like Eisenhower and MacArthur became heroes and then charismatic leaders. Clearly, someone who is respected and trusted by others is most able to exert influence over them.

The way to lead people beyond the limited capacity of more conventional power forms, and even beyond themselves, is to study charismatic power and then learn to use it ethically. I'll describe how to be charismatic later. And you needn't feel uncomfortable at the thought of wanting to be respected and admired, for increasingly, scholars are concluding that this urge relates more to the need to accomplish high goals than ego gratification.

People simply want to agree with and to follow charismatic leaders (often twisting their own logic to agree with a leader's position). Followers will defend a charismatic leader when he or she is not present, and will take strong exception to those who unfairly criti-

> **Charisma Can Be Dangerous**
>
> Adolf Hitler is a clear example of the amorality of charismatic power. Hitler took a depressed Germany, found a common relatively defenseless adversary (the Jews), and through the magic of his personality, was responsible for more evil than anyone in the 20th century.

cize the leader. (Some "friends" won't do that.) People who follow charismatic leaders are convinced that things will get better, whatever the condition, and they always feel better about themselves.

The Charismatic Leader and the Five Power Forms

The most effective leader is one who combines charismatic power with expert power from a legitimate power base, adding carefully measured portions of reward power and little or no coercive power. For their part, the followers subordinate their own interests to those expressed by the charismatic leader. In so doing, a symbiotic relationship is set up in which followers translate visions of the leader into their existence. The personal influence coming from charismatic power both complements and exceeds the impression made by office rewards, penalties, and expertise.

Charisma can often produce results without calling for other more common methods of power. Most people want to cooperate and to be part of an exciting and potentially significant activity. They seek a mission in

> ### What Business Needs Is a Few Good Marines
>
> The secret to charisma for the average guy is a combination of the conventional transactional power forms—the ability to reward or punish, position legitimacy and expertise, and be empowered by the organization. *Forbes* magazine (December 2000), in an article on how Silicon Valley could be saved, used the Marine Corps as an example which incidentally included all of the five power forms.
>
> The Marines are considered the most effective fighting machine in the world. There are seven levels in the hierarchy between a fire-team leader and the colonel commanding a regiment. The corporal commanding the fire-team, however, is empowered to make decisions on the spot and in the process given both authority over his team members and unusual tolerance for errors. As one moves up the ladder, there is less tolerance for errors and more authority until finally reaching the regimental commander who is distant, almost God-like, and is allowed from little to no room for being wrong. The entire hierarchy is peppered with expertise (intelligence): corporals and colonels are given special schooling and outside consultants are used on everything from tactics to decision making.
>
> The result is an empowered and informed organization that can change and act faster than its competition, and it always wins.

life beyond their personal lives. The leader who takes advantage of all the dimensions of rational charisma provides this mission. The duration of your influence depends almost exclusively upon your ability to use charismatic power.

Effective leadership is more rooted in charismatic influence rather than in more formal and traditional factors. Charisma is as effective among highly sophisticated groups which assume a peer relationship as among the less so. Indeed, often members of their groups will go to ridiculous lengths to gain your acceptance.

Bear in mind that followers will be especially loyal if association with you seems to offer a chance to enhance their own reputation or status. It is a wise leader who provides opportunities for reputation building.

Remember also that you can be perceived as charismatic more easily from a distant vantage point. Thus, the value of the podium, the stage, and the movie screen. Charismatic influence is more effective in structured rather than unstructured situations, that is, in formal rather than informal conditions. In unstructured settings, attractive personal qualities are less likely to influence behavior. Structure firmly sets limits and priorities, and establishes positions, further reinforcing the importance of your legitimate power. Assuming your legitimate position, you can become more personal. However, structure must come before familiarity. In the analogy of St. Simone, the key is, with warmth and familiarity, to reach down from the platform and bestow a meaningful contact. Just don't get off your platform.

An imprecise mission tends to yield to a leader a comparatively high degree of influence and control over group behavior. Under these conditions, even if you fail to achieve specific goals, people become more accepting, display higher satisfaction, and maintain support for the leader. Vague but lofty goals are good insurance for the leader. Others will follow if they perceive you as both important and somewhat mysterious. You will need measurable goals and specific objectives, but these should be subordinate to your quest to be the very best at whatever you are doing. These conditions should be laced into any of your input into long-range or strategic plans.

These, then, are the five forms of power: coercive, reward, legitimate, expert, and referent or charismatic. Your influence will be totally dependent in the extent to which you understand, develop, and astutely use a sensitive combination of these power forms. Know that by far the greatest of these is charisma, the ability to inspire trust and confidence, and that a charismatic presence can best be developed from a strong base of legitimate and expert power. So always make the most of your position and never stop learning your trade. In the following chapters, we will more carefully consider your path to charisma. During stressful times, you may want to reread certain chapters that have been particularly helpful.

- Power is often more smoke and mirrors than anything else.
- Always behave as if you were immortal and as if society were eternal.

The Development of Charisma

If you would be powerful, pretend to be powerful.
—Anonymous

To establish oneself in the world, one does all one can to seem established there already.
—Francois de la Rochefoucauld

How glorious it is—and how painful—to be an exception.
—Alfred Musset

In skating over thin ice, our safety is in our speed.
—Ralph Waldo Emerson

What is it that makes one person more magnetic and appealing than others? Why is it that certain people immediately inspire support, while others with equally good ideas in positions of equal authority fall short? The answer is charisma. And charisma, used with thoughtful measures of legitimate and expert power, a sprinkling of rewards and little to no coercion, will be your passage to the stars.

How can you develop and use charismatic qualities? Despite popular opinion, there is nothing genetic or intuitive about it.

Anyone of reasonable intelligence and high motivation can develop charismatic characteristics. Age, sex, race, height, weight, and other obvious personal characteristics have little or nothing to do with the ability to develop and use charismatic influence. Almost anyone who so desires can do it. You can do it.

> **Women**
>
> Having women at the top of a company can improve the bottom line. So says a study, "Wall Street Likes Women" by Theresa Welbourne of the University of Michigan. She found that higher numbers of top women managers improve stock prices and earnings per share.

Many factors contribute to charisma: sincerity, appearance, goodness, confidence, intelligence, foresight, wisdom, courage, thoughtfulness, kindness, control, vision, reliability, and so on. After reviewing virtually every published study on the subject, I have concluded that these traits fall under three principal categories: *distance, style* (charm), and *perceived self-confidence*. The most clearly documentable of the categories is distance—social distance.

The Importance of Social Distance

Although it may seem at first to be an uncomfortable concept, the most certain requirement for charisma, distance, becomes more acceptable as you understand it. Day-to-day intimacy destroys illusions, as anyone who has had a love affair knows; the relationship may survive but on more realistic terms. This daily contact, consequently, makes charisma more difficult to establish at the lower levels of most organizations. The man or woman immediately above you, with whom you work and talk every day, may have many strengths, but the frequency of contact obscures the strengths, displays weaknesses, and reduces charismatic impressions. That is why your closest associates, in the long run, offer the greatest single test of your leadership. Distance means being utterly transparent but remote, being everywhere and nowhere, being a friendly phantom. Distance means showing up where you are least expected. Distance means never telling your personal problems to those you would influence. Distance means having a close associate say after ten years, "Yes, he is my closest friend and I would do anything for him, but I still don't completely know him." Words like mystique, amorphous, magical, and inspiring should apply to you. To the extent possible, you should try to appear on important occasions and to be present often but briefly in the workplace. Remain sufficiently remote to enhance charisma.

On a personal level, you may find the concept of distance distasteful. Anyone deliberately using such a stance for personal advantage might seem calculating, even dishonest. How can it be right to be less than open, less than completely sharing? Aren't trust and confidence rooted in complete revelation and the exchange of intimate feelings? The answer to these questions is *no*, not if you want to lead or inspire others.

For you to admit full personal parity with those you would influence invites uncertainty, anxiety, confusion, and often chaos. Families, nations, congregations, companies, classrooms, and relationships have been destroyed for want of respect. Although respect must be earned, it is also a product of values, tradition, and privacy. It is best sustained through distance. The parent, teacher, or any leader must maintain enough closeness to promote understanding, but enough distance to be respected. This is because familiarity often breeds unproductive controversy.

Group Decision Making?

One of the most difficult things for owners to do is admit that they have neither the skills nor the desire to lead. That's what happened at Candide, an Internet company in New York's Silicon Alley. Six talented people joined together and agreed to share the power. It didn't work. The six partners finally decided to appoint an outsider as CEO. Everything from the working environment to the bottom line improved dramatically.

Distance is essential, for it allows those at the various levels in an organization to maintain reasonable order and ensure progress. The effective charismatic leader maintains optimal psychological distance. The leader is neither close enough to be hampered by undue emotional ties nor distant enough that emotional contact is lost.

You must find this balance for yourself. Remember, however, that you are more likely to err on the side of overly familiar. Look at religious leaders, for example. One minor lapse in conduct can jeopardize the image created as a moral, thoughtful, and controlled leader. Successful leaders will not allow an office to be devalued, either by themselves or by others. If you exceed the bounds of propriety in the presence of such a person, the demeanor of the effective leader abruptly negates this depreciation.

Distance has characterized effective leaders throughout history. There needn't be anything dishonest or unethical in distancing. Unless you are absolutely, unimpeachably wonderful (and you are not), it is unwise for you as a leader to establish intimate relationships with members of the organization you must inspire. Of course, you will be tempted to test this precept. But you will be exceedingly fortunate if those indiscretions don't come back to haunt you in the course of your future decision making. Be careful.

Distance is recognizing that you are no longer "one of the boys or girls." It is being a friendly presence: warm and genuine, concerned and interested, but rarely around too long or overly involved. Distance recognizes and uses the trappings of office, adjusting them only to suit the personality and sophistication of the audience or constituency. Distance balances remoteness with familiarity. You appear both exceedingly mysterious and utterly known.

Distance involves being warm and attentive, open and casual, but never, never getting off that platform with anyone who knows you by position.

As long as you realize that you are not really very different, except in

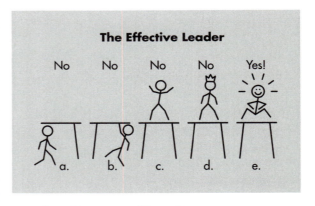

perspective, from anyone else, distance will not become arrogance. From time to time, aware leaders laugh at the reassuring thought that they are so insignificant. There is also a practical reason for this: The leader who takes the image too seriously or becomes overly self-serving will soon be found out and less effective. A lack of sincerity or commitment seems invariably to show itself to those you must inspire.

The message here is that if you lose interest in what you are doing, leave. The more you try to conceal the truth, the more transparent the lie. Apparently, the greater the motivation to lie, the less attention you pay to nonverbal clues that eventually give you away. You simply can't cheat for long and be effective.

You must remember that the connecting force between you and your followers is an emotionally charged relationship. Leaders are idealized as those whose strength enables them to assume the responsibility for their followers. Who else can better devise solutions and direction? In their idealization, followers deny that leaders experience doubts, insecurities, or weaknesses. Followers react to their leaders' human foibles with disbelief, astonishment, dismay, and even anger. It's as if they are saying, "If you are not totally dependable, then you may not be dependable at all." Charismatic leaders may drop their reserve safely only with intimates who accept their humanness and who have no motive for placing them in idealized positions or roles of omnipotence.

Note these points from research:
1) Social distance relates positively to productivity.
2) Distance between the leader and followers strengthens the group.
3) Low social distance creates tension.
4) Distance results in better communication in the organization.
5) Participative leaders are the least influential.
6) People are more secure with a strong leader.
7) People are more productive when roles are clearly defined and responsibilities are slightly overlapping.

Overlapping Responsibilities

Franklin Roosevelt was the first to deliberately introduce overlapping responsibilities in the federal government. He felt that in introducing an element of ambiguity and competition the performance of his lieutenants would be greater. He also believed that the resultant uncertainty would enhance his power and leadership effectiveness as he would sometimes need to be called upon to referee. The key is to exercise overlapping like a virtuoso—not too much or too little.

8) People perform better when they like and respect the leader, and social distance leaders are better liked and regarded.
9) The higher the perceived status of the leader, the more likely the group is to revere and accept the leader.
10) Leaders who are highly visible but operate less intently in the organization, yet retain final authority, are more charismatic.

Even with this evidence, there are still skeptics. A president of a distinguished college reviewed my previously mentioned book, *Power of the Presidency*, that addresses this subject. She wrote that the book was "fascinating, and instructive but somewhat perverse," and she absolutely refused to acknowledge the research premise for the assumption. I understand her problem. I know that distance may be an uncomfortable premise for you also, but don't abandon it without trying it or having sound evidence that you should follow another course.

A little self-disclosure by a leader will likely do more harm than good in sharing personal problems—too much socializing with fellow employees and telling or laughing too enthusiastically at jokes. Don't let them see you sweat is more than a slogan. Save full personal disclosure for close personal friends and loved ones, but be cordial with everyone. When you offer personal anecdotes, you compromise your status and reduce your effectiveness. People expect you to be superhuman, to be far superior to them. Remember this, just don't believe it!

Personal Style and Charisma

Style is a related characteristic that distinguishes a leader from the pack, but not so much as uniqueness. There is not as much evidence of its effectiveness as there is for distance and, therefore, it is a more debatable characteristic. Style combines many things—comportment, attitude, speech, dress, mannerisms, appearance, and personal habits. It's a kind of easy charm which is discussed in a subsequent chapter. Style is that fortifying inner sense that allows you to be individualistic. Above all else, it does not pander to every popular appetite and fancy, or attempt to be all things to all people. But style is also having sufficient confidence to say occasionally to yourself, without checking with closest advisors, "To hell with them; I'm going to be myself." Your advisors may think this is a lapse in discipline at first, but only you can judge when you should elect to follow your personal style; it's a balance of integrity and potential effectiveness.

It is true that with great legitimate power, a person can convincingly affect almost any style, regardless of how singular. For instance, many very successful people can often get away with peculiarities in behavior or dress. This may also hold for distinguished professional/author/artist types. But it rarely applies to organizational executives, except possibly those of long tenure and exceptional accomplishment. You shouldn't chance it. You must earn respect, confidence, and admiration first. Then, if you want, add the eccentric style as a distinctive signature.

Perceived Self-Confidence and Charisma

Perceived self-confidence and charisma is the third quality of the charismatic leader. It relates to a style of speaking and even walking. Remember the research on forecasting discussed earlier, that one who confidently predicts the future, even though sometimes wrong, will continue to be followed.

Effective leaders appear so confident that they are willing to appoint close associates who are superior to them. Usually there is no choice, for leaders need such associates to buttress their grand and confident generalizations. And you must do this! You are simply not that smart. Surround yourself with superior people, delegate authority to others and hold their feet to your stimulating fire, but never lose sight of the fact that you have the final responsibility. Behave confidently, but always know that you remain the same vulnerable person you were as a child on your mother's lap.

Charisma Is Not Classic

Charisma comes in different tones and styles. The key is for the leader to be a part of but apart from others, to be distinctive.

Jack Welch of General Electric made GE the most profitable corporation on the planet. Welch was a combative, go-ahead, take your best shot, kind of guy. Ted Turner is known for his flamboyance and candor. Bill Gates has been called a "latter-day robber baron." He is said not to suffer fools at all and to discover them through empowerment. Warren Buffett, of Berkshire Hathaway, another of the wealthiest men in the world, is said to be "magical" and to "delegate almost to the point of abdication." The late Roberto Goizueta whose final and perhaps most remarkable accomplishment at Coca Cola was that "Wall Street never blinked when he died." And Michael Eisner, of Disney, has been gunned at by shareholders, and in the process, raised profits by 25%.

There are psychological factors that may affect charisma. Leaders who are charismatic often become magical symbols. Followers will perceive you as having attributes that can advance their particular interests. Charisma not only depends on lofty goals, but to some extent continues (or replicates) dependence on a parent. The two conditions necessary for this identification are the perception of authority and the reassurance that comes from association with the leader. Each of these, however, are products of the leader's effective use of distance, style, and perceived self-confidence. *They enable the leader to symbolize hope and advance the interests of the people.*

Diminishing Charisma

Charismatic qualities tend to diminish with time. The charismatic role becomes increasingly difficult for many reasons. The most important one is increased familiarity with colleagues. Most leaders cannot maintain indefinitely the distance necessary for maximum leadership effectiveness. Time and experience tend to reduce the mystique. As people come to know their leader, they find in the leader a reflection of their own doubts, uncertainties, and limitations. So they are less likely to be as supportive.

While there are a few exceptions, seven to ten years in a particular office is about the maximum possible term for effectively exerting charismatic power. Contrary to popular belief, the smaller and less complex the organization, the shorter should be that term. People will come to know you faster and better. There are exceptions to this rule, but the wise leader rarely gambles on the long odds. Typically, after seven to ten years, the charismatic leader must increasingly rely on other forms of power, which is a sign to consider moving on.

Unfortunately, many leaders who have passed their peak effectiveness tend to rely on legitimate or coercive power instead. In other words, they merely give orders that increasingly may not be obeyed. As a result, they often resign or are forced out of office. This is unfortunate because it compromises what had been a stainless record. But once charisma is lost or on the wane in a particular setting, regaining it in that setting is almost impossible. The wise leader makes plans to move on long before the glow is gone. You can then move to another setting and start the same process all over again following one success with another. Assuming you have a genuine interest in the next position, you can be even more effective.

Charisma, then, usually is the most significant form of leadership. What you must do is, to the extent possible, gain each of the other power forms and from that base apply the characteristics of charisma. And you must apply them as a virtuoso plays an instrument—thoughtfully, gently, yet enthusiastically.

All of the forms of power discussed in these chapters are effective to some degree. From the most to the least effective, they rank as follows: charismatic public presence (referent, heroic), expert, legitimate, reward, and coercive. You should recall that the drive for power and influence often is only slightly less intense than the need for food and shelter. We all want to be somebody. The only variation is one of degree.

I have translated the sometimes uncomfortable subject of power into a leadership style employing all the power forms. You should remember that all of what follows is rooted at least loosely in the empirical research on power and leadership, and that power and leadership are one.

- Imprisoned inside us all, a confident, bold person is struggling to get out.
- Goodness, graciousness, likability, affability, but distance.
- There is a winner's aura that surrounds a person of good spirit.
- Be a friendly phantom.
- Give all the credit and take all the heat.
- You never have a cold, a headache, or a bad night.

Leadership and Power

For a man to achieve all that he can do he must regard himself as greater than he is.

—Goethe

The greatest mistake you can make in life is to be continually fearing you will make one.

—Elbert Hubbard

The minority is sometimes right; the majority is always wrong.
—George Bernard Shaw

To succeed in chaining the crowd you must seem to wear the same fetters.

—Voltaire

Yes, but it helps if you're tall and good looking.
—Lou Costello

E ffective use of power is the most important determinant of effective leaders. In this chapter I want to explain how leadership and organizational behavior are closely tied to power and how, from this understanding, you can be an influential effective leader. Outstanding leadership rests exclusively on the ability to acquire and use the various forms of power and one or more of the power forms include all of the many definitions of leadership. Those few who know and use power effectively are extraordinary leaders and run very successful offices and organizations. The others—the great majority—do significantly less well.

Leadership is the ability to acquire and use the various forms of power to inspire desired action in others. Researchers continue to speculate and debate about trait or situational leadership. Trait leadership depends heavily on a person with particular characteristics; situational leadership derives from an unusual convergence of conditions. In reality, most leadership is probably a combination of the two. But for your purposes, it doesn't matter. When done thoughtfully, you can lead in virtually any situation you choose. Indeed, in your work you are always in the right situation at the right time; if not, you should change your situation. Remember, you cannot lead if you are not prepared to be unloved at least by some. This doesn't mean you like being unpopular or that you won't try to correct the situation, you will. If what you are doing is important, you must be prepared to suffer rejection, at least temporarily. But always consider every adversary a potential ally.

Remember that in difficult, stressful situations, strong, active, obvious leadership is always more acceptable; in good times be more careful. So choose your situations carefully. For instance, you will become a leader more quickly in a troubled corporation than in a healthy one. And it's always wise to replace a person who was not considered effective on the job. In the broader context, current conditions set the moment and can help create favorable circumstances from which it is easier for leaders to emerge.

It is important you believe that leadership ability is *not* an innate characteristic of the privileged few. We inherit only a potential for nur-

The Death of Chrysler

After Daimler bought Chrysler, the value of Chrysler went from $37 billion to $2 billion. Apparently, Daimler didn't realize that it was the people who counted. And the top people left. The leadership was the heart and spirit of Chrysler. And when they left, all that remained was old factories and problems. When Bob Lutz, Tom Stallkamp, Francis Castaing and Tom Gale were pushed out, Chrysler essentially died.

turing and developing it. As with charisma, anyone who is reasonably intelligent and highly motivated can cultivate a successful leadership style. So, anyone can learn to use the various forms of power. Paradoxically, there is evidence that those of exceptionally high intelligence have more difficulty becoming effective leaders than the less endowed. This may be true because they have difficulty identifying with those they would lead (more on this later).

Although the word "leadership" is of relatively recent coinage, people possessing leadership characteristics date back to the origins of mankind.

The Importance of Leadership over Management Techniques

No company has ever continued to be profitable without strong leadership. Which is why many American companies are dropping initially attractive management techniques like TQM, re-engineering, matrix management, consensual decision making, and flat organizations. All fail without strong leadership. These leaders have made a difference regardless of process; leaders like Carly Fiorina of Hewlett-Packard, Douglas Ivester of Coca-Cola, Bill Gates of Microsoft, Jack Welch formerly of General Electric, Andy Grove of Intel, Herb Kelleher of Southwest Airlines, Michael Eisner of Disney, Ralph Larsen of Johnson & Johnson, Warren Buffett of Berkshire Hathaway, and Raymond Gilmartin of Merck.

(Power is much older.) History is written around these leaders. The Reformation is a the story of Luther, Calvin, and Zwingli. The American Revolution focuses on Washington, Adams, Franklin, and Jefferson. The French Revolution is about Voltaire, Robespierre, Danton, and Marat. And the Russian Revolution is about Lenin, Trotsky, and Stalin. So it is today with our business, political, military, and educational leaders. So it can be with you if you desire it badly enough.

Are You Leading or Managing?

The more you are able to act like a leader rather than a manager, the faster you will rise in your work and personal life. If you want to succeed in modern society, corporate or otherwise, you must be more than a manager. You must take the initiative. While good management is important, it is not leadership. And when you start thinking that it is, you are only signaling the end of your rise up the career ladder. We do not need dictatorial "experts,"

"Rocky" type jungle fighters, or completely conforming uncreative organization types.

What is the difference? Wherever there are problems, leaders arise to

Managing Versus Leading

During a self-appraisal at the midpoint of his presidency, Jimmy Carter criticized himself for managing the government rather than leading the country. By that time it was too late. Ronald Reagan, Bill Clinton, and George W. Bush have been leaders, not managers.

show the way, inspire, and persuade. They are the risk takers. Leaders speculate and make judgments—they make decisions. Managers carry out those decisions efficiently. (A manager can be completely efficient and still go out of business.) The very behaviors of the two types are antithetical.

Too often, the more management is studied, including in our most distinguished graduate schools of business, the greater the odds of not becoming a leader. It is so easy to become mired in the techniques of matrix management, strategic planning, collegiality, technical rationality, the rational model, TQM, re-engineering, or whatever the current rage, that you compromise your leadership

effectiveness and corporate action. Study these techniques, know them, and use them, but know that a leader does not stay at that level. Even in the new age of technology, the higher you go on the career

Leadership Versus Management

Harvard's, John Kotter, believes that most companies are under led and over managed. Managers do what was done yesterday better; leadership produces constructive change. Managers draw up budgets and long-term plans; leaders establish direction through a vision of the future and develop strategies to achieve that vision.

ladder, the less important is technical knowledge.

Managers implement ideas and policies and solve problems. They use rational premises or an established policy for decisions. They are analytical, fair minded, and have a strong sense of belonging to the organization. Managers often concentrate primarily on process. While leaders are often analytical and always fair minded, they are the organization rather than just a part of it; they embrace the organization as it embraces them. Leaders take chances, are visionary, and often act out of intuition with a high tolerance for ambiguity and paradox. Managers are more deliberate and careful; they equivocate. Leaders are dynamic and confident. When a crisis comes, they make a firm choice. Their decisions often seem based on serendipity and intuition rather than analysis, though indeed they have been carefully thought out. Managers work within existing variables; leaders tend to extrapolate. Leaders are speculative and inclined to make decisions based on intelligence, high hopes, and dreams—albeit with at least one foot based in reality.

Management can be learned, and contrary to much conventional thinking, so can leadership. And remember, effective leadership is understanding and using power. Power techniques will work equally well in both professional and personal life. Indeed, the two always relate. There has never been a highly successful human activity, in war, politics, business, or education that has not been affected by strong leadership.

You should cultivate and demonstrate leadership characteristics from your first days with an organization, no matter what your position. Do the same in personal relationships; don't consider work as a burden. You'll miss the learning, challenge, and opportunity found in it. Be

> ### See at Sea
>
> Patrick O'Brien, one of the most distinguished writers of our time, wrote 17 books around the character Jack Mabry as he moved from midshipman to admiral in the British Navy in the 19th century. As Mabry moved through the ranks, he was transferred from ship to ship and expected to modify his behavior consistent with his new roles. When he finally made captain, he was given a small private cabin, often ate alone, and was entitled to be piped aboard. He became even more respected; from this point, his eccentricities became admired and emulated and he went on to a brilliant and fascinating naval career.[1]

different from the mainstream professional in your organization— but not too different. Rarely be assertive and strong, but never blindly. Unless pressed, do not react quickly to a controversial subject. Successful people are often described as very self-confident, impulsively dynamic, often dramatic, and at times, unpredictable. If they are happy, they are also considered good and able to empower others. A consistent and reliable productivity seems to balance this changeability. Create an atmosphere of change and excitement about yourself. You must appear obsessed by your vision. Be unrelenting about your ideas or dreams. Excite, stimulate, and inspire others to work harder and more creatively. At work you should be driven by slogans like: "More, better on less," or "There is always a higher mountain" and "Quickly show a profit, whatever your bottom line."

Expect to make mistakes—action oriented, transformational people always do. Why? Because they are leaders and see themselves as risk-takers rather than managers. When you are acting out of both expertise and intuition, you're bound to make mistakes. Mistakes, however, can be invaluable if you analyze and learn from them. To dwell on your mistakes is self-indulgent and destructive. You will be the better for these experiences, and those who are with you will see your humanness and often feel more warmth toward you. But continue on in your bold style.

The Leader Sets Limits, Establishes Formats and Rules, Is Directive, Dilutes Business with Humor, Has a High Energy Level but Doesn't Stay Too Long, and Is Rarely a Genius

Contrary to popular belief, directive leadership is more effective than non-directive. The collegial concept doesn't work well, even in universities, where it has lead to almost complete stultification. Collegial decision making only works in a condition of individual accountability. Short of bankruptcy, a faculty senate suffers no consequences. Indeed, Max Weber wrote that collegiality was the highest form of elitism. In business this is typically called consensus decision-making, TQM, or re-engineering. Such practices tend to make the end product little more than maintaining the status quo. This was the problem at Silicon Valley and in other businesses where unique ideas gave rise to immediate profits only to stultify from poor management and inability to change.

People seek an astute, strong, assertive leader who involves them in the decision-making process. This person seeks and respects their ideas, but makes the final decision and accepts responsibility for it. This runs counter to most popular notions regarding corporate leadership.

Consider with some reservation the advisor or writer who has never held a top executive position (scholar or not) or one who has, but has only achieved a mediocre record. You must be especially careful here because such people are often top executives of established, but soon to be floundering, organizations. Or they are professors at distinguished universities who have never really been under fire. You should trust most those whose judgments are based on successful experiences or solid replicable research. Expect to learn from the person who has a current record of impressive performance or whose words have endured at least 200 years.

Highly visible leaders who do not overly involve themselves in the details of their organization, but who retain final authority, are more likely to be effective. They are also more likely to realize desired organizational structure and goals. Clearly, one purpose of a leader is to maintain organizational stability and responsiveness. Other studies suggest that group members do not develop or accept group norms and expectations unless they are well defined by leaders. Too much informal or familiar behavior on the part of leaders tends to reduce their perceived legitimacy. The overly folksy supervisor may soon become one of the folks again. The ideal combination is familiarity but always from the executive platform. Whatever your position, don't be overly familiar or invite excessive familiarity.

Norms or policies become more acceptable the longer they are in force. Leaders under such circumstances tend to be more readily accepted. So don't be too quick to change the rules unless they have become badly eroded over time. People seem inclined to accept conditions simply because "that's the way it's always been."

People expect their leaders to try to influence them. A leader who simply tries to reflect the wishes of a constituency or who declares neutrality on many key issues is evading responsibility. The leader must do more. After establishing a bond, the leader then begins the process of moving forward (transformation). People are rarely satisfied with echoes.

This is especially true during a

It's Leadership, Stupid

The CEO shapes the destiny of the organization. The selection of the leader can be life threatening (the two CEOs at Apple before Steve Jobs returned) or life saving (Gordon Bethune at Continental Airlines) or life extending (George Fisher of Kodak) or transforming (Lou Gerstner at IBM and Michael Armstrong at AT&T).

crises. Disruptive behavior, antagonism, tension, and absenteeism increase under poorly defined and nondirective situations. People, including the sophisticated, want and need structure. An informed leader knows that if a majority opposition coalition develops, it may undermine effectiveness. And the coalition itself may informally assume the leadership position.

What's more, people want and need credit for their accomplishments. The more effective leader invariably attributes competence to followers. Give them the credit while you absorb their stress.

Yes, effective leadership does seem to involve certain personal characteristics: A sense of humor, loyalty, above-average intelligence, extroversion, and boldness or willingness to take the initiative. Recently, other characteristics joined the list: Courage, fortitude, and sensitivity.

Researchers have also found that years of experience in one leadership role may not relate to the effectiveness of leadership as measured by productivity. There appears to be a point of diminishing returns for most leaders—a point in time after which they lose effectiveness; my estimate is seven to ten years.

Researchers have found that the physical characteristics of a leader are not as important as earlier studies had reported, nor are race and gender. Donna Shalala, President of the University of Miami and one of the most distinguished leaders in higher education, is former Secretary of Education and Chancellor of the University of Wisconsin at Madison; she is short and obviously female. The democratization movement of the period obviously affected the popular image of leaders. While being a tall, attractive, white Protestant male is not a disadvantage in achieving leadership, these characteristics, no longer seem to give a distinct edge. However, the typical CEO of a U.S. corporation is still male Protestant, usually educated at a state college, with an advanced degree from a name school such as Harvard, Stanford, or Northwestern.

More recent research suggests that leaders have or appear to have inordinate reserves of energy and stamina, and maintain unusually good physical condition. Even leaders handicapped by physical disability or poor health usually display great vigor. The effective leader always appears to have energy left over, and never complains of being tired, having a cold, or working too hard. Indeed, effective leaders work hard because they love their work.

At the same time the leader perseveres and copes well with stress. The leader's personal characteristics and values must seem to fit the needs and aspirations of the people. The effective leader pays attention to clues, questions, or the lack of them, others' body expressions, and other physical characteristics.

Researchers once believed that socioeconomic background played a significant role in creating leaders. While coming from a good family doesn't hurt, a remarkably healthy number of top executives come from poorer and middle-income backgrounds than from the wealthier classes. Religious and ethnic backgrounds apparently remain a significant influence on upward mobility within formal organizations. But the educational level or type of school attended seems to offset drawbacks caused by socioeconomic, gender, or racial factors.

Women executives, who were once in middle management, have found it more difficult than men to rise further. (Once they understand the use of power, they move more quickly.) However, a number of studies suggest that once in office, effective leadership is more a function of power and style than of gender. My own research suggests that the style of the leader is clearly more important than race or gender. For women, the key is to get there and throughout the course attend to the ideas presented here.

Hewlett-Packard on the March

Carly Fiorina, the current CEO of Hewlett-Packard and perhaps the most powerful women in business, says that "Power is the ability to change things." And she wields it like a warrior. She believes that to change a company you have to operate on the whole system: the strategy, the structure, the rewards, and the culture. She immediately changed Hewlett-Packard's decentralized system to an accountable hierarchy, and the company began to transform itself with essentially the same top people!

What about the relationship of intelligence to leadership? Early studies find that leaders who are much brighter than their followers are less successful. Later studies found that leaders whose intelligence is consistent with followers are more successful than leaders whose intelligence scores were either low or very high. More recent studies find that leaders are only *somewhat* brighter than their followers. Think of Truman, Eisenhower, Reagan, and the two Bushes.

Intelligence, as measured by verbal-ability tests, appears to relate to first level supervisory performance. But the higher you go in the management hierarchy, the less significant the correlation. Intelligence does not appear to be a real predictor of success at top levels. Indeed, a survey of effective executives to identify those who were most effective ranked high intelligence and logic the last two of 13 related characteristics. There is evidence, however, that leaders usually have superior judgment, decisiveness, knowledge, and fluency of speech.

Although the elements of chance and timing undoubtably play a part in the rise of individuals, the newly appointed executive today should know that effective leaders generally have these qualities: a strong drive for responsibility, loyalty, vigor (or its appearance), persistence, willingness to take chances, originality, ability to delegate, humor, initiative in social situations, fairness, sensitivity, self-confidence, decisiveness, sense of identity, personal style, capacity to organize, willingness to act boldly, willingness to share the credit for successes and absorb most of the stress of failure, and tolerance of frustration and delay (a quality undoubtably induced and fostered by the advent of bureaucracies). The aggregate sum of these qualities make up a extraordinary capacity to gain and use power.

This completes the first four chapters. Their highlights should be seared into your brain. The remainder of the book applies these principles to your organizational success. You may read them in sequence or as you prefer. Read on.

- To have nothing on your mind is far worse than being in trouble.
- The best statesman is not he who is the greatest doer, but he who sets others doing with the greatest success.
- Make as many changes and debatable decisions as possible during your honeymoon in office. It will establish a design for change, create precedent, and be accepted. Don't take seriously the person who says, "wait till you get the feel of the place." It's too late then.
- To accomplish goals, use anything within the limits of ethics and reasonable propriety, including cajolery, flattery, and persuasion.

- He who decries immodesty is twin to the statue that wears a fig-leaf.
- Beware of those who trumpet their achievements.
- Those who were disloyal to your predecessor will be disloyal to you.

Values and Power

Tact consists of knowing how far to go in going too far.
—Jean Cocteau

Three signs of a rogue: interrupting during a story, vicious-ness in play, and telling nasty jokes.

—Anonymous

The secret of being a bore is to tell everything.
—Voltaire

Many get the name of being witty, only to lose the credit of being sensible.
—Baltasar Gracian

Truth generally is kindness, but where the two diverge and collide, kindness should override truth.
—Samuel Butler (II)

Whatever you do as the main occupation in your life, you must consistently try to be the very best—the cream of the cream. There is no false claim in this desire, nor is it poor psychology to set high standards for yourself. It is more important to you than your ability to reward or punish, your expertise, and even your legitimate authority.

Most people have a mental image of themselves as average, and they will act according to this perception. On good days, they may think they are somewhat better, but if this persists, it triggers a reaction in which they feel awkward and guilty. After all, we are not supposed to be better than others. This is the person who explains errors by saying, "after all, I'm only human," or "I did my best," or the poorest excuse, "I'm sorry I didn't meet your high standards." You should constantly strive to be the best, not just good or better, but the best. During difficulties, you feel somewhat less, but if this "average" mood or self-abnegation lasts long, shake it. Move back on to your high course. It is axiomatic that most high performers judge themselves more harshly than their severest critics do. How much wiser it is for you to give a

> **Be the Best**
>
> Jack Welch was passionate about GE's being number one, almost ferocious in his drive to be the best. His vision was religious in its fervor. He was never satisfied. He never felt his dream was fleshed out. He moved through "Gotta be Number 1" to "Speed, Simplicity and Self-confidence" to "Boundary Lessness" to "Sigma Six." Yet, there was always more for GE to do. He once said, with a tinge of scorn, "Some CEO's think the day they became CEO is the high point of their careers. They ought to feel they are just beginning."

little understanding to yourself when you are faced with challenging tasks than to berate yourself while surrounded by many average performers. Which is happier? Which is more successful? Which is more powerful?

It would be arrogant and inappropriate to think you are better in all things when you are expert in just one or a few. For instance, when I was a CEO, I firmly believe that I was first-rate. When I meet another CEO who is as good or better, I am caught between mortification and inspiration, but the feeling is always uncomfortable. I am like the athlete who, upon being bested in the field, returns to the gym and starts working out. I am this way about what I do best. I do not apologize for expecting myself to stay at the front or with the frontrunners. Indeed, accomplishment without a measure of egoism is hypocrisy. I knew I was among the best in my field based not on fantasy, but on a continuous monitoring of my impact. I attempted to honestly count, weigh, or measure the poetry of the workplace. For me to deny my success would be false modesty. It is true that in two offices over the better part of two decades, I must credit my

> ## Arrogance and Fear
>
> After only two years, Doug Ivester was pushed out as CEO of Coca-Cola. It was reported as a tenure laced with arrogance and insecurity, a man who was blind to his own weaknesses, who would not take advice, and who was increasingly isolated and obsessed with controlling the smallest details. Ivester was considered a brilliant man who failed to grasp the most vital quality, leadership.

associates for most of what was accomplished. But I was certainly committed and things changed and were measurably better for everyone involved.

On the other hand, I am a fair to good poet and a bad painter. I am a good tennis player, writer, and speaker, and a serious psychologist. It does not bother me at all to read a better writer, to hear a better speaker, or to play a better tennis player. I do not presume to be the best in these things, although I appreciate the finest. I travel hundreds of miles to see an excellent art exhibit, watch a good tennis match, ask a great mind a question, or listen to a distinguished psychologist. I gladly have my writing edited and my backhand critiqued—and I am better for it. I am not uncomfortable. I am not the best in these things, and I have some skepticism about anyone who claims to master more than one pursuit.

Surely you can aspire to be the best at *something*! Be chief in something. It takes only some ability and a highly disciplined motivation with just a touch of luck. Believe in yourself, for there is no one else over whom you will have such certain control or on whom you can count when in difficulty. You can be so interested in a particular area that your career will choose you. If you must decide, pick something for which you are reasonably suited. Set yourself on an upward course, although you cannot see completely through the clouds. Know that at times it will be hard. Never be completely satisfied because this engenders inertia and stagnation. Stay on course.

Your Production Will Be Your License to Anything (Almost)

I cannot overemphasize the importance of exemplary performance. It will determine your lot in almost all things and at every level of the corporation. It will be your license to being controversial, to pressing yourself into affairs that appear to be beyond your ken, to having or appearing to have all of the five power forms, and to advancing to the top. This will be true even in a heavily bureaucratic corporation lead by managers who got it that way and who don't and won't see their error. Nonetheless, they sense it even though they may not grasp it sufficiently for their own good. They will not stand in your way. Rather, they will smile in appreciation and tolerance and grant you passage. Translate all of your activities into production. Perform those that meet this measure and eliminate the others as quickly as you can. I refer to such things as committee meetings, corporate politics, and most business social activity.

For instance, if your firm exists primarily to sell products, your every behavior should be defined in those terms, regardless of your assignment or how apparently important another role may be. Other jobs may be necessary and important, but none so important as sales. Quality control, market research, public relations, development, administration, finance, and production are all important. But without sales, they don't exist—without the delivery of the product to the consumer, the whole enterprise totters and finally falls. (This condition holds unless you are involved in government or other publicly sponsored enterprises. Even here you will rise faster if you are oriented toward the delivery of services.) Don't ever fall into the trap of believing that any assignment is as essential as sales, the effective presentation, and the delivery of your product.

It is really so simple to rise in a corporation following this premise, but few see it. If the function can't be defined in some way in terms of the delivery of services and ultimately sales, then discard it. If you're in no position to do this, then do your best to gracefully get another assignment. The path to the top in most companies is usually through sales. Whatever your special training (engineering, management, public relations, and so on), try to get a full-time sales assignment. It's like being in frontline combat. You will either win your medals on the firing line or miss this vital experience. The key to your success on the line will be knowing your product, boldness, action, and service performance. For instance, in banking, the loan function is where banks have made most of their money. If you haven't done this and done it well, you're probably not a future bank CEO.

Your personal power will grow in proportion to your sales. Wherever you go in the company, that early sales performance will be an indelible standard—your decoration and entree to speak on any subject. Just don't speak too often or too much. It's the solid foundation of the excellent teacher in the university who becomes the dean, or the admiral who has actually been in a sea battle. I am not saying that having done these kinds of things makes you superior. On the contrary, there may be too much significance attached to being at the scene of action. I am saying that your rise to the top will be significantly helped by experiences in the trenches, even if you did not win a hero's medal. If such experiences add to your luster, you needn't feel you have to apologize because your role was ordinary. Your advance will be based on performance, but the record of service never detracts and may represent potential power to your superiors.

Self-Discipline Is the Primary Trait of the Would-be Powerful

Now that you have read this far and know and appreciate the essential features in your quest for power and happiness, you are ready to combine the glue that holds your design together, *discipline.* Discipline is the controlling force that makes you stay on your platform when you crave closeness. It provides the strength that keeps your mouth shut when you feel impelled to speak prematurely. It keeps you from ordering a drink at lunch and enables you to say no. Discipline controls social distance with precision. Discipline is essential to charisma.

> **Moderation**
>
> Aristotle said, "Moderation in all things." Cary Grant at 81 said, "Moderation in all things except lovemaking." Take whichever you will, but remember that through moderation you can lead the good and full life.

The primary rule of your life should be discipline. For you, it is strictly administered. For those under your leadership, you benevolently but firmly apply and require it.

Without discipline, you could accomplish little or truly ever savor anything. Without discipline, all of the things I have outlined for you are little more than cocktail conversation to be replaced by the very next book you read. Discipline is the medium from which most worthwhile things spring. A person who seeks any excessive amount of gratification becomes overindulged and soft. The desire to unduly pamper oneself is antithetical to your interests. Undoubtably, you will be tempted to test this for yourself, and it isn't unwise because mistakes are an effective but frequently painful way to learn. So even when you have plenty, hold some of it back so that you can enjoy more fully what you have.

Persistence and concentration are the essence of discipline. They endow you with the ability to continue when others quit, to hang-in rather than hang-up. They allow you to say "no" when you're tempted to say "yes." Don't seek and then abandon your goal when your course seems tortuously slow and painful with, "I have a lousy boss, so I think I'll quit." Do that a few times

My Boss Is So Dumb

Bill had a promising future. He graduated with honors from Occidental and took an MBA at Harvard. But Bill was always smarter than his boss, or so he thought. And, he simply could not keep his judgements to himself.

After ten years, he had been with four companies and is now an anathema on the job market.

and the problem is not your boss's, it's yours. Handling difficult people is an art not only in business, but in life in general. Many individuals create and invite misfortune by their attitude. They are always looking for the next abuse, big or small, and are rarely disappointed. They develop neurotic complaints more quickly than do the optimistic and generally happy people. These malcontents are models of future failures whose downfall comes from a psychological egocentricity and lack of discipline.

The end products of your discipline will be an extraordinary richness of life containing order, neatness, patience, positive results, health, harmony, balance, excellence, control, power, love, and even good poetry. Discipline in your life reinforces the strength of these desirable qualities. You will really know excellence.

Those who work for you, who must trust and believe in you, whom you must inspire, must also have discipline. All people need both structure and form. Discipline implies respect for your co-workers, and the expectation that they will perform to high standards. You must let them know what you expect of them by clearly establishing and demonstrating certain rules of conduct. Periodically evaluate them but spontaneously note positive actions and reward them generously. Within these guidelines, give them their heads. They will invariably test your commitment to your values. Be pleasant and consistent, but firm. Do not let the slightest violation of your reasonable rules pass because the thought of confrontation is uncomfortable to you. Remember, life is a conflict between reason and nature, and reason doesn't win by accident.

Do these things without becoming one of them, and they will produce beyond their highest expectations. They will even surprise you, their ever-pressing leader. It will not be because you possess magical qualities, but because you have brought sensible order and form to their work lives. They will not only produce for you, but will come to admire and depend on you and invest you with charismatic qualities. Some may even love you and say, "Working with him has been the best experience of my life."

You must never be the one who checks on details, time-cards, or hands out petty reprimands. Someone else should monitor these details. Praise good work and appear to ignore the minutiae. For instance, if you are the manager, let an assistant manager carry most of the bad news. Focus on large issues, not the details of operations because you are above such things. If you are not high enough to enjoy such delegation, then be very restrained in the course of your delivery. People do not long respond to negatives.

Your self-discipline must extend to every facet of your life—from work to social and private life. From the time you wake in the morning until you retire at night, discipline should be the strongest thread of your day. The ability and judgment to say "yes" and "no" to the right things is a full-time exercise. For example, you must say no to staying in bed or otherwise wasting your day off. You don't really need that much sleep anyway, that is, if you have moderate habits, so get up and live. Occasionally go to the office on your day off. Do daily aerobic exercises, which can boost health and self-esteem, and require a regular schedule, at least 40 minutes, four times a week. I suggest aerobic as clearly preferable to isometric. You look better and last longer. Do something thoughtful for someone else as a reinforcement and reward for good performance. Do nice things for those who can't give you anything in return but appreciation. Those will be the ones who will support, even when you're wrong. Don't try the tempting foods of the day, from doughnuts to McDonald's to cocktail hor d'oeuvres. It becomes easier with practice. Do read that good book you've been wanting to read, and don't go out with friends who naturally want you to adapt to their bad habits and to continue throughout the evening with them for inadequate reasons. Don't look much at television, the greatest escape for non-thinkers in modern society. I am not suggesting you have all work and no play, but that you judge carefully when to act and work and when to relax and enjoy.

Now think about it, wouldn't you feel much better about your day off if you met more people of similar tastes and enjoyed the company of equally worthwhile people, or how about cultivating people a notch higher than you in taste. You would be easier to live with, happier, healthier, infinitely more productive, and always growing.

Neurotic people are ultimately disappointed in the relationships they establish with others. Is the other person at fault in these maladaptations? What do these neurotics expect of themselves and others? You will encounter such people in an unhealthy work group that frequently coalesces in the workplace. Those people reinforce negative behavior. It is a test of your improving self-control to deal with such people. To avoid them is to evade the issue. This challenges you to fine-tune your own judgment in discerning how to profitably relate to them and help them in the process. The extent to which you master the intricacies of dealing with pessimists will determine how successfully you manage your life in every phase. You can't ignore them; they are everywhere. Your personal stability and professional success will depend on it. Don't let others drag you down; you pull them up.

Now that I've said these things, let me reiterate the point that you must strive to be reasonable and moderate with yourself and others. Complete self-discipline is what you should strive for, although you know perfection is only an ideal and unattainable. But your life should be reasonably well-disciplined if you seek stability, personal happiness, and success. Self-discipline and frequent self-evaluations will let you know if and when you are slipping. When you are, the first temptation may be self-recrimination. Indulging oneself in a guilt trip is another lack of discipline and harmful. Instead, learn from the experience so you don't repeat it. You may not exercise every day, but on the days you do, you'll feel so much better. It results less in a physical sense of well-being than in an enhancement of self-esteem. The same will be true when you choose a low-calorie fish over a heavy meat dish at dinner. In no other areas of our lives is discipline and sensitivity more essential.

So it is your job. When you go early and stay late as necessary, concentrating in between, you will be amazed at how well your sales go, or your mind works, and how rewarding and productive your day is.

Hard Work

Cindy, the daughter of a self-made successful CEO, married Richard, an easy-going man of inherited wealth. One evening Richard, in an inspiring mood, asked Cindy the "secret of her father's success." Cindy answered, "I don't really know, but he was usually the first in the office and the last to leave." Richard never asked the question again.

It works because a disciplined, intelligent approach inevitably provides measurable results.

Most people won't use this logical approach, and are puzzled by their dismal results. This is where you will have the edge. You will produce more, advance more quickly, look better, and win more often because the positive results are self-reinforcing. And they become easier and more effective with experience. Hold your back erect and your stomach in. After a while, proper posture will be second nature. Most will talk this game, but they will reinforce only their verbal performance, and their talk will be as vacuous as their performance. Such people will never know what just a few steps more would have brought them. This is the way of the undisciplined. They eschew discipline and replace it with self-indulgence. All structure in their lives crumbles with time and easy pleasure. They finally warp from imbalance or fail totally in their important goals—professional and personal—for want of discipline, which requires strength. The self-indulgent pursue the same goals, desire the same ends, but are unwilling to submit to voluntary discipline. They chafe against authority. When they do not achieve their goals, they blame anything and anyone except themselves.

So you must above all things, hold to your discipline. Your self-control allows you to gauge precisely how much work and how much play to expect of yourself. You will be able to look back on a day, a year, or a lifetime and say, "By and large, it's been a good life," and know confidently how it was done and who was responsible.

Charm, Manners, and Charisma

Charm and manners are elements in personality which, combined with production and discipline, enhance your ability to succeed. Today, not enough is written about charm and manners in relationships. In the past, more time and effort were devoted to how to behave than how to produce. It was even taught in school. In effecting a balance, we've gone to the other extreme. We scarcely emphasize form and conduct, so most people neglect its importance. Those who are charming come by it through associations with alluring people and through trial and error in personal relationships. There is no formal base in society from which you can develop comfortable and acceptable social skills. Charm is an extraordinary and impressive congeniality you develop in interpersonal relationships—a code of conduct from which you work. Charm and manners are typically do-it-yourself acquisitions, and you should not be embarrassed to need a primer.

For instance, you are on a retreat sponsored by your company and receive an evening social invitation from your president. Dress is listed as "optional." What should you wear? A dark suit, a white, plain-collared shirt, dark tie and black shoes, of course. A woman should dress correspondingly. So it really didn't mean optional at all. Those who dress formally will have been asked expressly to do so by the host (usually a part of some program activity) or will be those who don't know better. You wear formal attire (and then it is always the most conservative) only when the invitation specifically designates "formal." It is acceptable for you to wear the same dark suit should you not have formal wear at hand. Here formal really means optional. A "formal" invitation means that you should still wear a jacket and tie, but in this case the jacket need not match the trousers. Insignificant? Don't think so.

A gentleman needn't be sexist to be courteous to a woman. A gentleman never leaves a woman alone, either sitting or standing until making sure she is comfortable and under no duress. He always rises or acknowledges in some appropriate way when a woman leaves or enters. When at the table, he never lifts a fork until the hostess does. If you don't already do these things naturally, then go out and buy a book of conventional etiquette that is at least 20 years old. Read it, adapt it to your personal style, and practice it.

These factors make up your operating frame of reference, your base of unofficial legitimate power. They determine how you practice it. They are compounded into the level of your charisma, which will determine how effective you are. From this established base, you can become the most charming rascal in your set. Now you have acquired the conventions of your society. You have a certain code of conduct, and you

A Few Words Go a Long Way

The scene is a meeting with Winston Churchill and Franklin Roosevelt during which Churchill hoped to get more lend-lease aid from the United States. It is reported that Roosevelt said later to Frank Knox that Churchill was the most brilliant conversationalist he had ever known; yet, after establishing the agenda, Churchill only asked Roosevelt questions about himself. Churchill got the aid.

dress distinctively, impeccably, and in good taste. More suggestions will follow on the important subject of dress. You are ready to consider the overall image you will project by considering the charm factor, that magical ability to create an impelling and lasting favorable impression.

Our informal world today may not often expect one to have civilized manners and to dress tastefully, but you will be the role model for others. Why risk your high goals on something as easy and uncompromising as manners or dress, which, in reality only reflect your regard for yourself. And you are exceptional. Remember, most assuredly, there will be those who will discredit you completely if you appear lacking in the slightest detail. Once you are adequately prepared, you will be able to relax completely within the expectations of social convention. Indeed, you are so at ease and confident that you occasionally bend or even break the rules under unusual circumstances. Do not do so often or arrogantly, but always with a graceful élan. You are now a pacesetter not only by knowing the rules but in knowing also where they do not apply. The response to your actions will be a measure of your ability to display charm.

Charm is usually more reserved than forward, more hesitant than pressing, is there even under trying circumstances, but it is always enveloping. Charm is a warm endearing smile, a subtle and gracious wit not overly used, a fluid manner, an ineffable lifting quality that is pleasing and reassuring. Charm is the heart of charisma, a major building block. Charm always engenders in others a feeling of enhanced self-worth and being uplifted. People always feel better because of you. The charming person

Charm Comes in Different Packages

In 1994, Herb Kelleher of Southwest Airlines was named by *Fortune* magazine as America's best CEO. On the way up he was more conventional, but today he is a prankster and kisser so unabashedly affectionate that his company's logo is LUV. He is so hands-on that he loads baggage and serves peanuts to passengers. He dresses in outlandish costumes and does crazy things, but all with a purpose. He is a pacesetter but he is invariably courteous and caring to employees as well as customers.

rarely says "I" except in the thousands of different forms of saying "I admire you" to the other person. Unless on stage, the charming person never plays to the group, but always to the individual, and even there, he or she speaks to individuals. The charmer's gently embracing attention is concentrated entirely on the other person, who is treated as an equal. This person is irresistible in that others feel uplifted by this respect. He or she constantly sincerely thinks, "How can I engage this person more effectively?" "How can I inspire this person to use his or her full potential for the program?" The focus is on that *one* person, always the individual. For that particular moment, the two of you are completely alone in a room filled with people. Empathy can be a loud, clear, and unique form of nonverbal communication.

Stay away from personal references to yourself. When asked a direct, personal question, answer succinctly, modestly, and humorously; turn the subject back to the other person or ask a question.

People love to be asked questions they can answer. Speak at length only when the topic is of compelling interest to the object of your attention. But here again, be cautious in using the first person singular. You don't do that without risk of sounding egocentric. There are ways you can ensure the subject chosen for conversation is one that is comfortable for you. At appropriate lulls in the conversation, you can casually interject a special interest of yours. "Oh, do you enjoy reading?" "What do you think of Paris?" "Do you enjoy tennis?" "The lovely view reminds me of a Thompson painting." You see, I know something of literature, Paris, sports, and American Impressionism. If the other person doesn't respond to one of those, I've got a range of topics I can throw in from Book VIII of Plato's *Republic*, which can be absolutely fascinating, and I can discuss country music, which promotes another dimension of human interest.

Most of all, the exercise of charm is enjoyable. You can't really be charming if you take yourself too seriously. There is a smile and an optimism in everything you say and do, and an occasional happy laugh. The laughter is always of the moment and directed at yourself or an inanimate object. It never devalues or degrades. There is always a cogent observation on the topic at hand. But charm is an entrancing subject. It has humorous aspects. You must always remember human frailties, especially your own. When you do so, regardless of the situation confronting you, you cannot help but be more reasonable with yourself and others.

Our tendency is to talk too much. Charmers are usually kinetic people and their movement inspires everything from wit to philosophy. It is only natural that an attentive and active mind is more productive than one resting on idle. Don't say every clever or profound thing that comes to you mind. Get your timing down so that comments achieve impact. A good rule of thumb is "one in three;" that is, use about one of three of your sudden flashes of insight. Try to for the most part, organize your thoughts before you speak, not as you speak.

Frame your ideas using good grammar; decide when best to use colloquial expressions; consider the possibility that what you say might be the wrong thing. Thus you will reduce retrospective self-criticism such as, "Why did I say that?" or "I could have said that so much better." Constantly try to upgrade your performance as long as you don't expect perfection. If you wait for the perfect

moment, rest assured it will never come. You'll find yourself thinking, "I wish I'd said that," or "If I could only have that opportunity again." Better to wish you hadn't than you had, for this is the
price of an active mind.

Take care so that when in full stream of your own poetic words,
you concentrate on the other person and do not shift from exciting
dialogue to a sermon. You may intend to convert the multitudes,
but you'll lose what audience you had. Don't pontificate. If you
find yourself distracted and not speaking effectively, be silent and
wait for a more inspired moment. Perhaps you are tired, or it could
be that your audience is inattentive and signaling you to stop.
Don't keep pressing. You'll just throw more wasted words into a
losing situation.

Charming people never whisper. Although they speak intimately, they never appear to be so bent on exclusivity that they
deliberately exclude others.

You should always tell less than you know in conversation.
Keep something in reserve about any subject, and especially about
yourself. Keep that air of mystery about yourself, for once undue
familiarity develops, your impact is permanently diminished.
Except for a precious few, you cannot be too careful about personal information or problems. The other person is not really interested in your problems anyway. Never complain of a cold, a bad day,
or a personal disappointment. As far as they know, these things
don't happen to you, or if they do, they have no real importance.

The charming person by definition is not loud, macho, crude,
vulgar, or glutinous. Did you ever hear of anyone behaving gross-
ly at a symphony? Play life as a musician would perform in a clas-
sical symphony—refined, stirring, subtle, and enchanting.

As I have said elsewhere, take care of your body in the best
Platonic sense. Give to your mind and body all of the beauty and
perfection of which they are capable. Get regular rest, eat the proper foods, and always leave the table hungry. Never drink exces-
sively, no more than one cocktail before dinner and only a small
sampling of the appropriate wines. Never drink at lunch.
Regardless of age or tastes, unless you are chairman of the board,
only drink beer at informal functions. If you do not drink alcohol,
then drink water, cola, or better yet, a tonic or mineral water with
lime or lemon. This makes you appear to be drinking without call-

ing attention to your preference. Best of all, don't drink any alcohol at all when you are "on stage"—which is most of the time.

You are careful about boisterous behavior in any setting, and the tendency is greater when you are in a group of the same sex. Often same-sex groups seem to build up a perception of exclusivity and immunity among them. Such groups tend to be overly loud, crude, and oblivious to offending others. Don't participate or remain long in such groups because your presence suggests support and

> **Be Careful What You Say**
>
> Remember Bill Clinton and Senator Kerry telling lesbian jokes at a New York restaurant? Were they simply telling tasteless jokes or revealing deep-seated feelings? Or George W's remark about a *New York Times* reporter that was picked up by a sensitive microphone.

insecurity and diminishes you even in the eyes of the participants. Be especially careful in groups when you are drinking. Stay dignified, graceful, and modest. If you can't maintain control consistently, don't drink.

Finally, practice your charm at home as diligently as at work or social affairs. Be charming toward those with whom you live. This includes your spouse, parents, friends, children, and servants. Be especially careful with servants. People who become overly familiar (not charming) with servants usually have to discharge them for overstepping their bounds. Although familiarity encourages disrespect, they tend to blame the servants. Think of yourself as a servant.

Your Humor Should Be Spontaneous, but Administered with Small Doses

Do not strive to be too funny or entertaining. Know that occasional lightheartedness and quick wit are evidence of a good sense of humor, but to be typed as a comic comes at the expense of never being considered serious or sensible. As you become established, you are tempted to display an easy wit. Being humorous and entertaining may make you more popular, but it will scarcely inspire trust and confidence. Let your colleagues and friends provide most of the fun. You provide the sense and a little fun.

This applies to social settings as well. If you must socialize with business associates, and occasionally one must, show a charm, but always be reserved. Keep a respectable distance so that you do not crowd, and you are not crowded. Remember, the secret to being a bore is to talk too much about your peculiar interests, to tell everything in endless detail. There is no such thing as a clever bore. You will never get into difficulty by laughing occasionally, smiling often, and saying little and remaining somewhat remote. Your reserve will lend to your mystery and your impact.

In creating a social circle of personal supporters, don't rely on jokes. The very word signals a bore in good society. Most jokes are for those who are too slow to display wit. People of taste never admire anyone who too frequently resorts to jokes. Let your humor be born of the situation. The moment gives rise to the laughter. It will also be a sign that you are both quick and spontaneous, delivering original conversation rather than repeating some ancient jest.

Don't be hesitant to initiate or respond to gentle humor in serious settings. It's a sign that you are comfortable and that you have a good balance between serious dialogue and tasteful levity. Don't do it to the extent that people view you as an entertainer. This is regarded as subservience. Guard against spontaneous humor that embarrasses or debases another person. It is aggressive and hostile humor that is easily recognized. Once you have hurt another, you will not regain his or her esteem regardless of how many apologetic things you may do or say later. This type of action ends usually in repayment in kind. Let your humor arise from the situation and be personal only when you know there is no chance for misinterpretation.

Frivolity should have little place in your work life. You should not even indulge in frivolous behavior during periods of relaxation. Frivolity by its very definition indicates you are unworthy of serious attention. It's precisely the opposite of the heroic quality characterizing you. You have the strength that abjures the insignificant, that stays on course in pursuing important goals. Use that intelligence in approaching problems, in organizing accurately, and seeing brighter visions. The results will be rewarding even if you are overly optimistic.

Ethics Augment and Maintain Power

Ethics is that consistently high standard of behavior that you maintain in all of your professional affairs. It requires honesty, decency, honor, and fairness in your business dealings. Sounds simple, but can you maintain such standards? Is it naive to espouse it, particularly in a book on power?

"Much read authors have written that the power seeker should try to achieve a goal without the slightest moral scruple. To such individuals, right is whatever wins or sells. Others believe in a double standard, that ethical behavior is required in their personal lives, but is a sign of weakness if used in their professional or institutional lives. They rationalize their ethical

The Unethical Mainstream

In Phil Porter's *Eat or Be Eaten* (Prentice Hall Press 2001) the reader is told how to chew-up subordinates, ruin rivals by rumor and accusation and make others pay for your mistakes.

Ethics: Richard Nixon and the Scranton Commission

In 1972, I was appointed to a national commission on student unrest by the Nixon White House. Nixon had reportedly been concerned about the report of another commission chaired by the Governor of Pennsylvania and the President of Vanderbilt University. He felt that report was too liberal and wanted a counterpoint report from a more conservative group of college presidents.

I was known as a law-and-order president; that is, I believed in the use of civil disobedience but with consequences. I was appointed to a national panel chaired by the Chancellor of the California State University System. After several months work, the Chairman sent a draft report to the panel. It was too extreme for me. I told the Chairman I could not, in conscience, sign the document, but that I had no intention of making waves. I suggested that I simply be dropped from the panel and agreed that I would make no public statements. Shortly after I was invited to the White House Blue Room for a meeting where my concerns were noted and the report changed.

I'll never forget the salute of the Marine at the entrance as I and my assistant, also a former Marine, pulled our car through the White House gates. As a result of the changes, the report never became news worthy, and three years later, the Chancellor offered me the presidency of San Francisco State University. President Nixon sent me a Christmas card each year for the remainder of his time in office. I still have a copy of that report.

compromise as being a personal sacrifice, but a necessary one for the goal. It's for the welfare of the company, the university, the people, or the country. State and corporate rulers repeatedly face the conflict of choosing between the best interests of the country or corporation, or placing personal integrity uppermost. If you must decide between a questionable professional practice and professional conquest, which would you choose? You should choose ethics, integrity, and honor, but it will not always be easy. Do not long consider another course, for a slight ethical lapse will finally become a hole in your soul."

Let's first look at a simple morality (an amusing proposition for the pragmatist). Think for a moment of a single issue—how many lives have been spent in the name of God? In similar fashion, how many times has hurt come to an individual because a superior has justified a decision as being "our" decision, in the best interest of a company or the state? Whenever we depersonalize others, we remove ourselves from moral obligation. We advance the glorious cause at the expense of injuries to the victimized individuals. But the moral dilemma scarcely inhibits those interested in a ruthless demonstration of power.

Plato held quite a different perspective. He believed that a power interest was a necessary feature of the good person. He was convinced that the powerful individual should be completely candid about a personal power drive. He also thought the person of power should be respected by society. Aristotle also spoke of power and ethics as being intertwined. And while Machiavelli believed that we are all motivated by self-interests, some to the point of depravity, he felt also that the power seeker could not achieve ends without commonly accepted ethical virtues.

Recent studies on effective corporations have concluded that, in the long-run, the most profitable corporation places the *individual* over the corporate interest whether that individual is a staff member or a customer. The effective corporation values service over profits and therefore makes greater profits. It's as if the effective corporation is saying, "If I honestly try to satisfy you, I'll satisfy my own need as well as make a profit." Or "If I please you, I'll be exhibiting my abilities to do so and, hence, my power." This is not inconsistent with rational downsizing. With a modicum of management expertise and ethical principles, your success will be assured.

In my own professional life, I have found that ethics and honor are both a comfort and a license. I am comfortable in the knowledge that my winning has resulted from an honest game. I have license, in that assuming an ethical base and a worthy cause, I have been completely candid in addressing both my goals and the condition of my enterprise. If my entire life were as pure as my professional life, I might be considered a candidate for sainthood. It has not been so, and the small ranks of saints are scant reassurance. My professional life leaves a residue that is far more than a good feeling. It indicates a method of structured living and achieving worthwhile goals rather than personal aggrandizement. I would not trade ethics and honor for anything, for they are indispensable accessories to the proper application of power. To subordinate your ethical standards for selfish opportunity is antithetical to the good person.

You will be tempted. Time and time again on your road to leadership, you will find what appear to be acceptable compromises offered in the most seductive guises imaginable. They will come from all quarters and at times when they are most welcome. Some colleagues offer personal intimacy in order to control you. Employees and others may offer excessive praise in looking for your vulnerable spot. Superiors may offer advancement and special perks to obligate you in the future. Experts will scrutinize you to see how you can be seduced. Be assured you are on the

> **If You Can't Generalize from the Act, Don't Do It**
>
> At Archer Daniels Midland, a key corporate officer participated in a price-fixing scheme from which ADM made millions. Later, he blew the whistle and the company was fined. He was damaged goods forever.

proper course if your professional establishment senses that it cannot compromise your ethical standards and shows a healthy regard for you as a significant force. As a kinetic person, expect criticism subtly expressed through rumor, gossip, innuendo, and abrasive humor. Don't try to defend yourself regardless of what they say. This gives credibility to your detractors. You fight for ideas, services, actions, others, and productivity in your business. In time, you will ethically enlist even your detractors. A rule of thumb from Immanuel Kant, "An act is probably unethical if you can't generalize it."

One question that arises periodically is how you proceed if you become aware that the policies of your establishment are outdated. How do you proceed to deal with this? You address it carefully by always addressing issues and practices, but *never* individuals. The responsible parties are obvious to all and no gain comes from a personal condemnation. If you take this approach, everyone can discuss past errors openly and publicize new standards. Your exceptional record of production underscores the new criteria and establishes expertise in your field. You need all of your charismatic skills and ability to inspire trust and confidence. Despite their disagreement with some of your ideas, your methods or timing, even your adversaries will be hard put to challenge your purposes, ethics, or results. Most will come to like and admire you because they realize intuitively that requiring ethical conduct is a major aspect of the strong individual. Unprincipled people are like chameleons—they don't differ from their environment. There is simply no advantage in being unethical; there is only short-term gratification. The long-term cost is to destroy your ability to inspire trust and confidence without which you are lost.

Therefore, you must be ethical in all dimensions of your business activity. One compromise casts doubts on your integrity that may be impossible to eradicate. There is an old saying that the clock that strikes 13 casts grave doubts on all previous pronouncements. Dishonesty is not an accident but rather a method of operation. Unethical people are the ones who spend precious resources, time or money on manipulation and other covert activities that wouldn't have been necessary had they not abandoned acceptable standards.

To be ethical, honorable and fair means that in good conscience you can enter any arena swinging. You can

Ethics

Senators Chas "Mac" Mathias, Republican from Maryland, and Paul Simon, Democrat of Illinois, were long serving members of the US Senate. Both were known as men of absolute principal and impenetrable character. Lobbyists and Senators were known to be wary of these two completely incorruptible men. Neither ever reached the apex of political power, although Simon tried. They simply would not "play ball." Yet, of all the elected officials I have known in fifty years, they are the two I admire most and remember best. I can hardly recall the others.

freely, without the slightest compunction, go out to win. You can be candid, controversial, tough, and dynamic. Your announced intention is to win, to exceed all previous efforts, to chart new courses, to elevate all that you touch. And you will.

- Let your conduct proceed from goodwill.
- Keep your honor sacred.
- Ethics above all.
- Production is your license to individualism.
- So long as people know you know better, you can break the rules of social etiquette.
- Take care of your people at all costs.

Emotions and Power

> *To gain power over people, depersonalize; to gain absolute power, depersonalize absolutely.*
>
> —R.G.H. Siu

> *Our enemies' opinion of us comes closer to the truth than our own.*
>
> —Francois de la Rochefoucauld

> *No disguise can long conceal love where it exists, or long feign it where it is lacking.*
>
> —Francois de la Rochefoucauld

> *Most people enjoy the inferiority of their friends.*
>
> —Lord Chesterfield

This chapter will consider the four basic emotions; anger, grief, fear, and joy. They will be considered in variation and together and on close conjunction with your personal happiness and success. In brief: Anger, like coercion, should rarely, if ever, be your prime motivation. Resist acting in anger or any of its variants: revenge, denigration, disdain, and hate. Grief is good for you in small quantities as are its derivatives, anguish and guilt. Fear is also of value to you; in small quantities. Joy and its companions, friendship and love, will be both the enhancement and the pain of your ascendancy.

The Joy of Power

Power should be a joyful experience. Once you know what it is and how to get it and use it, you must develop special, and omnipresent pleasure in its exer-

Could this Be You?

A short time after open heart surgery, I fell into a deep depression. My usual upbeat, confident nature was lost in a tidal wave of despair, guilt, and worthlessness. During the depths of those months, nothing, absolutely nothing, was sustaining. Although I was a trained psychologist, I had never really understood depression. I had no answers. I saw Dr. Paul McHugh, Head of Psychiatry at Johns Hopkins University, the most gentle man I have known, and with the help of medication, I survived.

When I finally emerged from this dark, deep well, I had a completely different attitude about emotional illness and the extent to which we can control our feelings and behavior. It was the most revealing and humbling experience of my life.

cise. There is nothing at all perverse in this. Exercising power for impact, rather than exclusively for your own glory, can be perfect joy. To bring to others advancement, happiness, and rewarding contribution is a happy wonder to behold and is a way to convince yourself that you are worthy as a human being. To know that your presence has accompanied people to heights beyond themselves is as humbling as it is wonderful. To watch others around you grow and exude a new and gentle confidence is to truly empower them. They believe and they are so much more than they were before you. Yet you know that it was in them all the time.

You must answer this idea of empowerment of others with everyone in your life, in your personal life as well as your work. They will always remember and what a lovely reward for you, but after you are gone, they must be able to stand alone, completely alone, independent, vibrant, giving, and empowering to others. And so the altruistic cycle continues.

This will be your additional test: the extent to which you can give up those you liberate. It will not be easy. Indeed, to give up such joyous company can be wrenching. There is some pleasure in being relieved of the pressure of more or less continuous inspiration, of now being able to go somewhere or be with someone with whom you can speak without dusting off your words, where you can be completely revealing of yourself and your innermost thoughts. But, nonetheless, to let them go in the certain knowledge that they no longer need you is a sadly beautiful thing. But you must do it. To cling to your influence over others beyond the point of diminishing returns in terms of their best interest is complete contradiction of everything you must be. The good parent knows this as does every corporate mentor.

So you will find great joy in power, both in its gaining and finally in giving it away. The emotional exchange as in idealized love discussed later, is two way, for you will love them also, you will trust one another completely and in adversity you are always there for each other. But remember in their eyes, you never really have adversity, you are theirs as an example, an exemplar; your reward comes in more subtle forms. By your confident, happy, strong behavior you teach them to do the same for others, and the only way you can really be perceived this way is to perform, for you must always remember that you are really no different than they.

Anguish Can Inspire

In small doses, anguish is good for those who aspire to power. It keeps charisma pure, and therefore, genuine and effective. In your desire to excel, you will make mistakes, for you have learned that while both are important, action exceeds contemplation. Anguish is the price you pay for acting too quickly, for not having contemplated or studied sufficiently. Another kind of anguish is born of your sloppy preparation, short sightedness, or just plain laziness, of your failure to maintain sufficient discipline. Or it comes at those times when you have compromised your professional ethics and personal honor. Here anguish is the necessary cure to prevent repetition. For this you pay a price, and your Freudian superego, your conscience, should send a heavy message to your ego as it wars against your damnable id, your totally selfish side, in the process. You will not only feel guilty, but you may also fear you'll be found out for the mercenary hound that you are. That bruised superego cries out in anguish. "Ah, what a horrible undoing." "Oh God, help me out of this one, and I'll never do it again."

One of the reasons that high principles serve as the best and most profitable course, is that in sloth and deceit, we are our own worst enemy. We think that what we have done is unforgivable and that the consequences, if discovered, will be disastrous. This may not really be so, but my telling you this will not change your anxious feeling. You will feel lousy when you don't do your best or when you have even tacitly engaged in a deceitful act. You won't sleep well; you will be preoccupied, snappish, and your appetite will fall off. But this will only be temporary.

In anguish, the first temptation is to wallow awhile in self-pity and rationalization. Denial and blaming others are a second resort. But eventually you will admit your indiscretion with genuine regret and then you must make repairs. And if you have offended others, you must apologize to those you have offended or wronged. And you must do so publicly before all who know of your action.

Public apology, however, need not always be in order. If your mistake has been in poor management, or inattention and poor preparation (laziness), then you can just be certain it doesn't happen again. To apologize to your superiors is only a guise for sympathy and forbearance in such cases. After a while, such people are considered weak and unreliable and are rarely considered for advancement. But if you have brought hurt or embarrassment to another person, then apologize and suffer your losses for there should and will be some.

When you anguish, you sear your misdeeds or mistakes on your mind and feelings as a tattoo on your body. Don't forget the lesson. Learn from your faults, and don't repeat them as most do.

But, how do you get back to the dynamic power stream from a state of anguish? As quickly as possible, honestly follow these steps:
1) Retreat to first principles which would be religious or moral;
2) Resist the temptation to excuse yourself;
3) Admit to yourself your mistake and regret your action;

4) Make repairs; and

5) Learn from the experience.

Now, stop there. Get on with your life. Things will be better tomorrow.

I will not presume to advise you about the anguish of being rejected in love except to say that the same principles apply. This is the most devastating kind of psychological pain. Should you become deeply caught in such pain, know that time will heal you and correct your self-defeating behavior. You may also want to talk to a therapist to attempt to understand better the factors that assail you. Here, most of all, try to avoid repetition of the same behavior in the future, but your consolation is that love is also the very greatest joy you will have. More on this later. In love or anguish, try to get your feet back on the ground as quickly as possible. If you continue long in such an obvious state, the one will make you a hopeless wimp, and the other a weak romantic. If you live a good and reasonably disciplined life, your love will settle down into a strong, warm embrace, and your anguish will pass.

One further bit of personal advice on anguish. A while ago, I had a heart attack while traveling on an airplane. I knew that I had one chance in two to be alive in 24 hours. After a moment's sheer panic, during which I said a quick prayer, a few "thank yous," and "I'm sorry's," there was not the least bit of fear. I advised the nervous attendants about how to negotiate the stretcher out of the small plane. I wasn't at all irritated with the emergency medical technician when he couldn't get the IV into my arm. And on the way to the hospital, I recall asking the ambulance attendant questions about where she lived and went to school and what she wanted to do with her life. Nor was there anything especially poetic about the experience—no profound words for my epitaph, no stirring eulogy. Just a quiet, undramatic acceptance of whatever came and a strong desire to do my part to stay alive. I recall thinking to myself during my convalescence, "If dying isn't so frightening, how can life, at times, be so bad?" It doesn't have to be.

The Use of Fear (Coercion)

Your subordinates (but never call them that) should view you with a certain respectful fear. This is that slight degree of coercive power that you imply. Remember that holding out the possibility of using authority (legitimate power) is infinitely more effective than actually using it. And the extent to which you, in your insecurity, allow your subordinates to bridge the distance between you will be the degree to which you cannot command respectful fear without actually using your authority. You should not allow anyone to close that distance, at least not anyone you would lead and inspire.

Occasionally, you must remind your able associates who is in charge. If not, they will disregard discipline and lose respect for you. Consequently, a good staff will go off in countless different directions. And it will be your fault, because you have not piqued their anxiety occasionally by reminding them they are not completely autonomous. This does not mean that you do not continue as their warm and smiling leader who is always courteous and kind to them. Rather, you are also the confident and alert leader who occasionally, particularly early in your tenure, tightens the reins at the most subtle testing of your authority and leadership. Do so infrequently, but when you do, be prepared to follow through; you will probably never have to.

You should rarely go so far as having to dismiss an employee. When you must, do it gently and firmly, leaving no doubt as to the reason requiring such action. Think about it enough in advance and gather sufficient data so that you will not allow yourself to be persuaded to change your mind in mid-course. Be fair, even generous in your separation arrangements and conduct them all in absolute privacy. Never talk about, in fact, don't ever mention having "fired" someone. It is a cheap word used by the petty, the insecure, or the tyrannical. The person will be gone soon enough and the indistinct awareness will subtly enhance the respectful fear that makes most such unpleasant episodes necessary.

You must not inject so much fear into your relations with staff that you compromise your ability to inspire. Always remember that coercion, though an effective form of power, is by far the least effective of all five power forms. The charismatic leader rarely does more than display the *potential* for strong action. If you use coercion, do so very rarely and in an exemplary fashion that establishes a principle. Its overuse is the last bastion of the failing leader. There is a delicate balance here and you must play it like a virtuoso. You will know if you're going off-course. It will usually be because you have been reluctant to admonish and inspire your associates in the first place. The natural thing is to want to take the middle road and only faintly do either. Don't be afraid to be firm. Used infrequently, coercion serves to reaffirm the corporate structure, restores discipline and harmony, and raises the standing of the leader—you.

True Friendship: Only a Few

Can anyone bent on power and success have close friendships? Of course. True friends will be necessary and precious to you. But don't expect to have many and don't expect too much. The person who believes he or she has many good friends is either naive or a fool. The person who claims many friends rarely has real friends. The energy and commitment required for a worthwhile friendship puts a limit on their number just as the demands of a loving relationship make them even rarer. Aristotle wrote, "The wish for friendship will arise in a minute, but true friendship takes time."

As you achieve more power, you will attract a legion of followers who will call themselves friends. To them, you will be funnier,

> **Don't Act In Kind**
>
> A CEO got into trouble. Although his actions were debatable, they were completely ethical. (In time, they even turned out to be profitable.) During his moment of jeopardy, he called to two old "friends" for help. One helped and the other gave him a lecture and backed off. The CEO never forgot. Interestingly, the "friend" who backed off came to the CEO a few years later and, without the slightest compunction, asked for a big favor. The CEO smiled knowingly and granted the favor.

better looking, wiser, and sexier. But don't take it seriously. One good storm, and most of them will run for cover. Count as rare that small handful who remain with you when you are besieged. But don't count as inconstant those who leave either. Instead count yourself the fool because you expected more. Laugh about it. Don't condemn.

True friendship will jeopardize your ability to employ each of the five power forms. Intimacy breeds debate. It opens your judgment to question. It puts you on an even footing, which is appropriate for friendship. Indeed, friendship is delightful, instructive, and quite wonderful. But in work, friendship can often render you completely impotent. Unless you are desperate or stunningly brilliant, a friend will usually want to debate your decisions. The good friend has seen you stripped of your trappings, and since rarely are we really desperate or brilliant, our friends will say, "Yes, but...."

It is the weak and insecure executive who succumbs too often to the temptation of friendship along the way. So it is with the teacher who places popularity ahead of respect and the parent who wants to be a "buddy." If you choose to establish friendships in your work place, and you very well may, then abandon all serious plans for rising in your organization. Even if you are promoted, it will take an inordinate amount of time and you won't be effective after you get there. Instant popularity and colleagueship are the refuge of the insecure. If you want to be one of the boys or girls, fine, (and I mean this), just don't expect to be anything more.

This does not mean that friends in your work place will always abuse you. But because of the nature of true friendship, they will have a right to, for once you give yourself in friendship you do not have the right to withdraw it easily. Next to family, friendship is your most important source of personal strength and the foremost obligation of your life.

True friendship, like love, is one of the rare, really beautiful things in life. It should not be granted easily or quickly, for, to do so will be never to know its true blessings. Even if you follow this advice, you will probably know at some time in your life the disappointment of being let down by someone you thought was a true friend. And even this should not end the friendship. You confront the friend and try to carefully resolve the conflict.

There is no joy like the sight of a friend (or the one you love). It doesn't matter if you've seen the person yesterday. To see a friend is to light all of your senses with warmth, acceptance, and love. Just to talk to a friend over thousands of miles by telephone

Bobby Knight and Me

The Council for the Advancement and Support of Education (CASE) was the largest organization of colleges, universities, and schools in the United States. In 1978, I was appointed President of CASE. In 1982, in a speech I said that "Intercollegiate athletics was the major hypocrisy in American higher education." Quite innocently, this speech coincided with Bobby Knight's "mooning" as he angrily boarded a plane in Puerto Rico. An article about the speech reached the President of Indiana University who immediately declared his intention to withdraw from CASE.

He then proceeded to place the prospect on the agenda of the Council of Ten which included all of the Big Ten presidents. I was nervous. My presidency could probably survive with the loss of Indiana University, but the entire Big Ten? I called two friends at Big Ten universities, one of whom was a life-long friend for whom I had been instrumental in his initial university appointment. Both "friends" lectured me that although they agreed with my position on athletics, I had been too candid and advised me to cool it in the future. I didn't know any other Big Ten presidents well enough to ask for their help. I remained nervous in office, backed by my conviction and the support of a shrinking group of CASE members.

The publicity mounted, and I received a call from Father Theodore Hesburgh, then the President of Notre Dame University. At the time I didn't know Father Hesburgh well, although I had always admired him. He asked about the articles he had read and what he could do to help. He told me that he would "contact the Big Ten." The proposal did not pass the Council of Ten and I never heard of the issue again. Later, I found out that, among others, I had also been supported by the presidents of the University of Michigan, Iowa and Ohio State, men I didn't even know.

My stock was higher than ever, but my relationship with my life-long "good friend" was never quite the same again.

can bring happiness. Your day is better and so are you. And when you are down or in trouble, a true friend is the greatest gift of all. That friend is in when you call and if he or she knows of your trouble your friend has already taken action. That friend supports you regardless of your disagreements. That friend does not judge or condemn or abandon you, but instead shows a determination to understand and respect your autonomy.

While there may be a subtle sexual message in this, friendship need not involve sex, that is, physical sex. Indeed, it is infinitely better if there is none, for then friendship is too easily subordinated to sex, that is, physical sex. Once the appetite is sated or sex is withdrawn, unless there is love (an extremely rare occurrence) the friendship is gone. Friends may talk and hug and touch but they don't cross the line. This can be really difficult for opposite sex friends. Resist the temptation.

Friendship requires that you are there. Dependability is the first requisite, that you offer your caring support under *any* conditions. This does not mean that you will always agree with your friends or that you will support them in efforts that you feel will hurt them. But whatever the test, you always love your friends. There is no condition in your love. Your friend need not be successful, important, or present. Your friendship is a denominator for virtually every decision you make regarding your relationship. For your friend, you would do virtually anything at almost any price. A very successful and happy man I knew well used to say, "A friend is the kind of person who will bail you out when you're guilty." He lived by that code all of his life and received great loyalty in return.

A friend is more than your cause, your institution, your company and yes, even your rise to power. So don't enter into friendship easily. There are, of course, more limited but nonetheless honest friendships, friendships that are both useful and true; colleagues, office friendships, and other situational relationships. These relationships can be deep and extraordinary but they do not cross the lines into other spheres of your life.

Because you are successful and in demand, there are many people who will seek your friendship. You certainly shouldn't dissuade them. Just be careful. When you are in trouble, and you will be, count as wonderful that small handful who will be there, and it will be a small handful. Remember always that it is your sacred obligation to be there for them also...whatever the price.

"Love" (Infatuation) Generates Power

Love is the most misused word in any language. Its definitions and use are so varied that only poets have come close to its meaning. In contemporary society, the word has been so abused that it can describe both a mild infatuation and a profound relationship, but whatever its intensity, love is power. Power is control. The full range of love grants control to the loved one. In its most undiluted form, love is not dependent on any of the five conventional power forms, although in its dispassionate exercise you can engage them all; that is, you can use the love of others to your advantage. Remember always, that in love of any kind, you are bound to the advantage of the other person as well as yourself. If you do not, you will become venal and despicable, even to your self.

Like religion, love is largely without reason. And it is not fully subject to rational analysis. Because of your charismatic nature, you will frequently inspire a kind of irrational adulation. That is, many will desire and support you without regard to your real merit. This is good so long as you do not abuse or mislead them. But this is not love.

In effect, these people do not love you in a full sense, they "are infatuated with who and what they think you are." Theirs is an idealized condition, that state where one person is so overwhelmed by another that the strong passions overwhelm all other considerations. The ephemeral quality of such relationships makes them fragile. Such idealization of one individual by another rarely fits into the world of reality. Really being in love is more nearly a feeling of the highest regard for another based on an understanding and acceptance of the loved one's intrinsic qualities, both good and questionable.

This idealized condition amounts to an adulation and an acceptance that can and does, occasionally, border on the irrational. When someone feels this way, you become godlike. Indeed, in one-on-one relationships, you will usually be turned off by overly close association with those who feel this way. And there may be many. It's that roll you are on. And know in such cases

Power Can Corrupt

The debacle of Bill Clinton's departure from the Presidency, coupled with the stains on his reputation inflicted by his personal conduct, are dramatic reminders that power does not absolve one of the responsibilities of using it ethically, judiciously, and incorruptibly. Clinton's horrific start as a private citizen tainted both his future and his Presidential legacy. His rise and fall are excellent examples of the importance of legitimate power to charismatic leadership. Think on it.

that it's the podium, the flair, the mystique. It's the stuff of heroes, of kings and queens; it's not really you. The mystique of social distance always inspires admiration and often, sometimes too often, love. You're making your way effectively. Just don't take yourself too seriously. Remember, groupies come in all shapes and sizes, from those who flock to rock singers to those who are irresistibly attracted to the rising star in the company. Be careful. Remember Bill Clinton.

Most charismatic types who are in leadership positions will say, during extremely private or unguarded moments, that they have never made a presentation in public where they haven't inspired some kind of irrational response from one or more members of the audience. Those responses come in all forms, from better job offers, to phone numbers, to room keys. Yes, this is a form of love, the weakest. Don't take it seriously.

This response is visceral rather than cerebral. It's like the magnetism between Philip and Mildred in *Of Human Bondage*. If you don't remember it, go back and reread it. You'll be reminded of what it means to be completely smitten. Philip became completely helpless. This kind of intense idealization empowers the recipient with a license to lead anywhere. In its milder form, this kind of adoration is akin to the sports hero in your high school who seemed to be able to do anything. And it will happen to you. Just don't abuse it. Remember, it comes from social distance, not intimacy. Typically, intimacy destroys it. An interesting irony.

This affection comes from both sexes. Both women and men will be attracted to you. It is not always sexual, although I am convinced that there are sexual undercurrents in all positive relationships between men and women. (Freud was usually right

The Twin Devils: Power and Sex

Rutgers's anthropologist, Helen Fisher, (no relation) suggests that there are biological differences between someone who drives him or herself to become a leader and someone who has only enough energy to drive to work. "There is no question that a high level of testosterone is associated with drive and aggressiveness, and also associated with the sex drive." She writes in the *Anatomy of Love*, "People, especially women, are attracted to power. Don't just assume that the man in power is constantly approaching; they may be approaching him."

after all.) These people who are drawn to you simply want to be in your company, to hear your voice and ideas, as well as to see you. To them, whatever you say is sparkling and profound (even on a down day). Whatever you write is seminal and however you look is perfect. You are loved.

This state differs from that in friendship because it can become so emotionally overwhelming that good judgment fails and is replaced by blind devotion. These people will do as you ask them without regard for any limitation, theirs or yours. You can do no wrong in their eyes. You must remember to keep your feet on the ground because such intense devotion does not tolerate errors easily, and can be withdrawn abruptly.

Obviously those who love you this way can be invaluable in your ascendancy. They boost your occasionally sagging spirits. They always give you a vote of confidence. In return, you can inspire them to performance heights that are completely without precedent. And the benefits inure to both them and you. This is the key to your own emotional balance in this kind of love. Whatever is done in the relationship must be to their advantage as well as yours, because they will follow you anywhere from the boardroom to the bedroom.

You can do everything to inspire this kind of adulation. It does not happen by accident. It's a combination of all the wonderful things you are. It's principally the way you combine social distance, expertise, and position (legitimate power). It reflects your sincerity and caring, but is not overly revealing. Your presence is constant but you are never possessed. You appear utterly open but somehow private, transparent but remote, genuinely friendly but fleeting. You convey a genuine personal attachment to each of your followers. Your idealized personage grants you power. People get caught up in your mission, your dream.

Because of your self confidence, your charm is spontaneous. This kind of adulation comes to you regardless of the other power forms. It happens in public places where people don't know you. It's your style, the way you carry yourself. Don't ever forget, however, that you can boost your charisma if you have the other four dimensions of power: reward, expert, legitimate, and even the implication of coercion. These power forms play an incremental part in the process and can serve to temporarily prop you up when you aren't completely up to form.

Should *you* love in its deepest sense? Even in its deeper hues, to love is to risk allowing yourself to be controlled, to show your caring completely and to be known offstage. What will she think when she realizes that you are not inherently different, that you are fallible and, of all things, subject to needing and giving love? I don't mean the so-called love of fleeting infatuation or sexual gratification on a casual level—but *love*. I mean love in the sense of regarding another as of ultimate worth and importance, of assuming the responsibility of enriching that person's existence at whatever cost, and of establishing an intimacy and sensitivity to the other that requires honesty, openness, and a continuous awareness of the condition in order to respond with sensitivity.

Most never know this love; they are too preoccupied, fearful, so concerned with themselves that they can't see the lovely beyond. They fall in love too easily, they use the word as a lubricant to pleasure and in the process miss the essence of life; the intense love of self- revelation, of becoming all but consumed by the thought of another and of risking yourself in its course. Yes, it is risky, but to have such love returned is the most completely beautiful condition in life. It is the sweet, sad love of Romeo and Juliet, the sacrificing love of the Duke and Duchess of Windsor. Yes, it borders on addiction even obsession, and you must tread its path carefully, but to walk it is to live and to truly love, and finally it settles into a lovely and constant course of trust, caring, comfort, beauty and occasional passion. But for you there may be one or perhaps two relationships in your lifetime that can enter with such intensity and total involvement. These relationships comprise the source for the caring that you extend to the larger group around you, and represent the extent to which you are willing, or able, to really test your true self in the eyes of a loved one, to show someone the real you. Yes, you really are vulnerable.

So you should love. Both the intense and finally comfortable concentration existing between two people and the constant attitude of caring, which can embrace hundreds, for love will make your life exciting and worthwhile. It's just that with one at a time love, you are off your platform. Pray that you love the right person.

- True friendship in work is questionable and love is beyond question.
- Never trust anyone who speaks well of everybody, but you speak ill of none.
- We forgive more faults in love than in friendship.
- If you want a person's faults, go to his friends.

The Care and Feeding
of the Boss

A man who is not a fool can rid himself of every folly but vanity.
—Jean Jacques Rousseau

Familiarity in one's superiors causes bitterness, for it may not be returned.

—Friedrich Nietzsche

Men are more ready to offend one who desires to be beloved than one who wishes to be feared.

—Machiavelli

The ultimate responsibility for final decisions rests securely on the boss. Your boss is always right. You have three choices when he or she arrives at a decision: support your boss, change your boss's mind, or resign.

Your Boss Should Be Your Mentor

In your desire to get ahead, don't allow yourself to name-drop or fawn over superiors. While it is proper and appropriate to compliment honestly, admire, and be supportive of your superiors, it is inappropriate to be obsequious and flattering. Bow to your superiors in worthy recognition and regard for their contributions and you will bow with grace and dignity. You'll know when you're going too far because you will feel a stress from bestowing unwarranted praise. Don't fabricate praise of anyone, including yourself. Don't seek favors, for this is a method of the weak. Work for what you get, and you can expect the same from others: actions, not lip service. There simply is no other way for people of strength. On the other hand, you should give deserved support to others. Do so as magnanimously as possible. So long as you do not compromise the power of your position in the process you will, in fact, enhance your power because support for meritorious people implies power.

Disagreements with Your Boss

Being loyal to your superiors in no way conflicts with your development or standing as a leader. Indeed, effective leaders have almost invariably also been first-rate followers. Your boss should feel that your skills complement his or her personality, that your talents offset his or her personal limitations, and that you are no threat personally because of your loyal traits. For these attributes, you will be granted latitude in your job, and recognition for your services and upward mobility. Do not jeopardize these things by splitting hairs over your salary, extra benefits or your office furniture. Remember you are beginning to build a power base and you shouldn't quibble over small matters. In time your performance will yield these things and more. Arguments are often decided on bad feelings and not logic, so don't argue with your boss. When you strongly disagree, think about it a while. Then state your position clearly but without emotion or puffery. Do it only once! Unless invited, it is usually unwise to pursue the matter again. You have done your task as a responsible staff member and future events will support the more accurate one.

Never state your disagreement with your boss in a group meeting or in any situation where your boss may be discredited. State significant differences only in person and when you are alone together. Think long and hard before disagreeing with your boss, making certain you can document an approach that will be better for him or her and the company. You want to be perceived as astute, but never in a way that shows a disrespect or belittlement of your boss. There are many unemployed bright people who do not know how to put their ideas across. Your job is to support your boss and produce. This is what you are expected and paid to do. Bear in mind also that the boss's ideas just might be better than yours.

Your boss is absolutely essential to your career. In fact, very few have risen without some kind of strong mentoring relationship with a highly placed person. Don't even think of going around your boss to complain or report to a higher authority. This leads to self-destruction. Don't respond to invitations from higher-ups to supply negative opinions, no matter how justified you may think you are in doing so. Ethical people would never ask you to become a collaborator.

The Weak Boss

Many young power seekers feel that they are working for weak bosses. Sometimes they are correct, but they receive a severe penalty if they're wrong. More often, they are too impetuous and judge the leader on inadequate evidence. The young new executive always seems to know how to run the entire organization. Whatever your reason, don't try to overpower your weak boss. If he or she proves to be weak, let others recognize this and the situation will be an advantage in providing you with opportunities for greater responsibility. So long as he or she's the boss, you can be cut right out of the organization. And a frightened, weak boss

Delegate Everything but Final Authority

The President of Harvard was too slow to delegate. He got swamped in detail and collegiality and became exhausted. After two weeks at home, he was still unavailable for comment.

will be the most vicious of all. Being weak, the boss may know little about the intricacies of the business world but is often an expert in hand-to-hand combat.

Don't circumvent your boss. If your boss is really weak, higher-ups will know it eventually and will come to you for confirmation. The approach to solicit information may be very subtle. Don't give evidence to them. It is hardly your job to be a hatchet person. So long as you work for a person, be loyal. If there are no good things to say about his performance, stay quiet. The next boss will note your remarks and decide how much he or she needs a judge around. In the long run, your comportment will be remembered and admired, because loyalty is a strong and desirable trait. You are not aiding and abetting the boss. You are remaining in your proper role. No one who is worthwhile admires disloyalty, in any shade or for any reason. Never take the seductive bait of catering to those who make surreptitious moves to discredit the boss. If you would betray one, you would betray another, and such a weak characteristic cannot pass unnoticed even if done in secret.

Should your boss be so insecure that your success is viewed as a threat, then offer reassurance. Be very open and leave no doubts as to your loyalty or motivation. The boss taught you how to sell. It was his or her ideas that were passed on to you. He gave you the benefit of his experience. Whatever you've accomplished, your boss is responsible for a portion of this achievement. In time, people will give credit where credit is due. You may pass by on the way up and still acknowledge your former bosses as having complemented your career.

Loyalty to Your Boss Is as Important as Production

Let's take a closer look at loyalty to your boss. Remember that in almost all situations, social and professional, people are observing you. As you become more productive, you will be noticed and tested under fire by a growing number of your associates. In time you will become a special interest to the top leadership in your company. Because you take pride in the quality of your performance, you will want to respond impressively to this attention. You may feel flattered and perhaps too anxious to please under these conditions.

Let's take an example: Assume that you report directly to a manager who has limitations (and who doesn't). At times, you disapprove of things that this manager—your boss—does. You believe that others are also aware of your boss's limitations.

Indeed, you know your unit could be more productive if your manager used other techniques or was replaced. The regional vice president to whom your manager reports has noticed you. The vice president admires your work and seems to like you. She talks privately with you, at first socially, and then gradually slips into business discussions. After a time, you are invited to share your opinion of your boss with the vice president. Ah, you think, an opportunity to impress the vice president and perhaps to rise more speedily in the organization. *Don't do it!* The motive of such an individual has much more to do with his or her promotion than with any concern about your welfare.

Unless you are prepared to resign, you should rarely share your critical judgment of a superior officer, even when asked, with another higher-ranking officer. It will be tempting. Your boss may be wrong about many things, you may even think that you are not being treated fairly. Don't speak unguardedly, regardless of the situation or your perception of the situation.

Again, to become an effective, charismatic person yourself, you must agree with your boss, change the boss's mind, or resign. If you speak to the vice president about your immediate manager, regardless of the rationale provided in order to get the information, in time your act will be branded as disloyal. If you would do this to one person you would do it to another using the

> ### Agree with the Boss, Change the Boss's Mind, or Resign
>
> John Lombardi led the University of Florida for almost a decade. He was popular on campus and his administration was marked by academic and financial success. National rankings went up, graduate school enrollment increased, and the endowment increased nearly five-fold.
>
> But his aggressive style led to run-ins with his boss, the Chancellor, and he was fired.

same rationale for your underhanded action. Even an unusually obtuse vice president can figure this out. You will not advance far in the organization.

How do you handle such a situation then? Tell the vice president you are flattered by his or her attention, but speak candidly of your feelings about loyalty in a professional setting.

Smile respectfully and keep producing. The vice president will get her information from other less astute people in the organization who do not recognize they are being used. And you will get the promotion.

Remember, don't be disloyal or display other weaknesses of personality. It is entirely normal to be tempted by an easy method to the top, but this is not the behavior of the powerful. By stressing loyalty, I do not imply that you compromise principle at all—issues, yes, principles never. After all, you have the option of quietly transferring or resigning.

However, don't resign until you have another position. It's almost impossible and always risky to find an equivalent or better position after you have resigned and have no legitimate employment base. While you are seeking other employment, don't explain to prospective new employers that you are looking because you disapprove of your present boss or company. Be more equivocal, for only an inept and weak person complains to an unfamiliar person. Consider that your prospective new boss may be thinking about what you will say about him or her should things not work out.

When You Are The Boss

When you are the boss, at whatever level, give due credit for your extraordinary production to your subordinates. They will respect your generosity in underscoring their vital contribution. How you address them is important, too. They are your associates, not your staff or your people. Again, they will appreciate your implied inclusion. Whatever is accomplished is *their* success and in difficult times you absorb their stress. This may be hard initially, especially when you have done the lion's share of the effort, but do it, in time you will be repaid many times over.

- You have three choices: agree with your boss, change your boss's mind, or resign.
- There is no excuse for not getting along with your immediate supervisor.
- Get to know your boss as well as he or she will let you.
- Invite the boss for dinner.

- In the office, come early, stay late.
- You are the boss, whether it fits comfortably or not.
- At least once a week, show up where you are least expected.

Changing Jobs

Every hero becomes a bore at last.

—Ralph Waldo Emerson

Fame is the beginning of the fall of greatness.

— Alexandre Rozanov

The best reason for changing jobs is to start doing what you should have been doing in the first place. You can't build power based on a checkered past. If things are going badly, you'll know within the first year. If this is the case, be certain that you aren't dissatisfied from either impatience or inexperience and then make plans to move on.

After you start your career, you can safely change jobs once every five to ten years. There is no resume so doubtful as that of the "job hoppers." If you haven't been promoted within four years, you've made a bust of establishing any personal charisma. You may have simply picked the wrong firm (but don't use this as an excuse too quickly). Seek another position.

It is acceptable for you to leave after three to five years for an obviously higher position. Generally, however, it is best to move up the ranks in the same organization for eight to ten years. Then move to a better situation elsewhere unless you are really extraordinary and on track for some exceptional post. With few exceptions, only managers stay forever in the same corporation; leaders move on.

In most situations, your charismatic potential will be pretty well exhausted within ten years and you will have to rely increasingly on your expertise. When that begins to run thin, you'll probably fall back on the power of your position, reward power, and some coercion. Neither of these will long serve you well. When you start punishing people or trying to buy them, it's time for you to quietly pack your bags. It will be only a matter of time before production drops significantly and you are found out.

Because you succeed and enjoy the respite from pressures and security, you will be tempted to stay with your organization beyond the point of your self-interest. Do this only if you want to homestead and coast the remainder of your career. This is not all bad. If after ten years your situation is secure and reasonably comfortable, and you have no driving desire to increase your power, then by all means stay. You may be happier in

Time To Go

Jack Welch left GE at the top of his game. GE was the third most profitable company on the planet, but most regarded it as the most valuable and America's greatest wealth creator. He was only 64, but he thought it was time to go.

the long run. Just bear in mind that the effective leader reaches a peak about the third year and stays there until the seventh or eighth. After that, charismatic quality begins to diminish and one can usually survive effectively for two or three years. Beyond this, you can continue to inspire others to greater achievements, although you will probably have already begun to rely unduly on rewards and authority. Of course, you may decide to accept less dramatic results. And, if your directors continue to be satisfied, as they usually will, you may continue tentatively for years. I don't recommend it.

Occasionally, there are truly exceptional leaders who enjoy dramatic effectiveness for two decades or more. They are the rare exceptions rather than the rule. To be on the safe side, don't assume that you are the exception. You have about as much chance of being one as you did being a player for the Boston Celtics or prima ballerina in the American Ballet Theater. You can be great for about ten years. After that, should you want to continue to dazzle, find another galaxy.

Bear in mind that I have said you may tire of the glow and choose another less tumultuous and demanding course. You can get tired of always being on a platform. Should you do so, don't apologize. Reaching the platform at all is a real achievement. The rest of your life will be the richer for having had the experience.

How to Seek Jobs

Regardless of any laws, good intentions or outward appearances, the "old boy, old girl network" still is usually the prime route for a new position. Simply stated, it's often who you know, or better yet, who knows you. That makes a difference in your job hunt. There are apparent exceptions in certain scarce fields, but after entering the field, you'll find exactly the same conditions at play. There are also those who find positions through a blind response to classified advertisements. But these instances are rare, and, almost always, the position is likely to be of a lower order than the one you now have.

Bearing in mind that production is your main key to a successful appointment and promotion, then personal contacts provide your access. Contacts, however, will only open the door. They will not obtain or keep the job for you nor will they get you promoted. I would state categorically that if you try to use contact after your appointment, you're dead. Don't even consider it. As your boss, I am not at all interested, except perhaps for business purposes, that Senator Smith or the chairman of the board endorses you. Indeed, you let me hear too much of this kind of talk, and I'll isolate you from any real activity or opportunity in the corporation. You are a potential danger to my control. You and I are the masters of our own professional destiny, not some other power figure.

Your contacts can help you gain access, however. Use them to call your credentials to the attention of prospective employers. They can do this by letter or phone call. Occasionally, your contacts allow you to use their name in making the inquiry yourself. The best way, however, is for the contact to recommend or nominate you for the position in which you are interested. At the very least, they can usually get you a serious interview. During this meeting you never mention the name of the contact unless his or her name is brought up in conversation by your prospective employer. Do not use the transparent strategy of using contacts as references. Unless the person intimately knows your work, don't list them, as this invites scrutiny. There are few things more damaging to your prospects than referring your prospective employer to someone who doesn't really know you.

If you have no contacts, then use the major newspapers and professional journals and make direct application for a position. You're more likely to do this when you're new to a profession than after you are established. From this point on, you should always try to structure your job search so that the prospective employer appears to seek you out. There are a number of ways to accomplish this. Just think about it. It is the rare person who gets a really good position after self-nomination. There is always someone else who will do it for you.

Executive Search Firms

During recent years, executive search firms have gained considerable prominence. In some respects, they now serve as a significant adjunct of the old boy, old girl system. So, there are some things you should know about them. Unless you have a close contact in the search firm, be careful about going to one seeking employment. Those eagerly accepting a cold overture from you will end up fleecing you. The really professional firms will not take you seriously. If anything, they will

Korn/Ferry International

John Kuhnle, a Managing Director of Korn/Ferry, says that most of the CEOs that he recruits are persons whom he contacts or who are recommended to him by persons he respects. He then likes to meet them, studies their resumes, and begins the process of matching them with the appropriate organization.

think you are too desperate for work and will not connect charisma to an individual dependent on others for placement. On the other hand, if a mutual contact sets you up, it is a different matter.

When officers of established search firms call you, take them seriously. They won't charge you anything. Their money comes from your grateful new employer. These firms often have excellent contacts and are seriously regarded by their clients. Once you become acquainted, even if a job possibility doesn't pan out, you will be remembered. In time, you will get calls about the most interesting and unusual prospects.

Your Resume

You will, of course, need a resume. It is also generally a waste of time to go to career counselors, employment services, or resume writers.

Your resume will get a close review. Resumes will rarely get you the job, but a really bad one can keep you from getting one and a good one can open doors. The bad ones use puffy adjectives describing accomplishments which shouldn't have been listed in the first place. List only your really important accomplishments and let them speak for themselves. Don't elaborate. Read this again so you'll remember it.

Regardless of what you've seen or heard from professional resume writers, do not use any resume form that calls for descriptive material. Be as objective and positive as feasible and list what you've done. If prospective employers want a writing sample, they'll ask for it. The length of your resume should be determined by your accomplishments and you should not add embellishments. Every notation should be self-explanatory and not depend on any preceding point. Do not be too politically correct; you may scare off prospective employers. In spite of contrary opinions, your resume should include such things as personal information (age, health, marital status), other work experience, travel and interests. These things color your resume with the real you and can enlist support for the most unlikely reasons. Under these conditions, your resume should be as brief as possible. A good eye-catching, efficient resume implying power looks like this:

Sample Resume

John Curtis Brant
984 Jackson Court
Washington, D.C. 22036
(202)327-5925 (Residence)
(202)842-5530 (Office)

Personal Data

Date of Birth:	June 2, 1958
Place of Birth:	Harrison, Illinois
Height:	6'1"
Weight:	172
Married:	Emma Kathryn Brant
Children:	Michael Carey (4), Brooke Elizabeth (2)
Health:	Excellent

Education

B.A.	1974	College of Charleston (Cum Laude)
		Major: English Minor: Economics
MBA	1978	Harvard University, School of Business

Professional Experience

1985 - present	Regional Manager, International Business Machines (IBM) Washington, D.C.
1976 - 1985	Sales representative, Assistant District Manager, District Manager IBM, Boston, Mass.

Other Work Experience

In school and college, worked part time for United States Post Office, as a tennis professional, in clothing and insurance sales, as a theater manager, and as a railroad section hand.

Awards and Honors

Several IBM sales and service awards
Who's Who in American Colleges and Universities
Phi Alpha Kappa (national English honor society)
Phi Alpha Theta (national history honor society)

Current Activities

member, St. James Episcopal Church
member, Board of Advisors, St. Stevens Preparatory School
member, Regional Alumni Board, Harvard University
member, Board of Directors, College of Charleston Alumni
    Divisional Chair, United Community Fund
member, Target Five Task Force, Regional Chapter, American
    Cancer Society

Former Activities

Sigma Chi Fraternity
Undergraduate Student Government
Varsity Tennis

Hobbies and Interests

Reading, theater, art, travel, tennis, golf

REFERENCES ON REQUEST

It will be your resume that was your first impression and this resume neither offends nor off-puts anyone; it is straightforward, complete, modest but telling. Some find it helpful to have a "brag sheet" that appears like a press release prepared by someone else. This could be included with your resume. Now to secure the position your strategy will include your contacts; your references, your past performance which shows promise of an even more productive future; and above these things, the personal chemistry between you and the person who will make the final employment decision.

The Interview

"You get a man through his religion and not yours." These words from George Bernard Shaw are fundamental to a successful job interview. After a good night's sleep, dress conservatively in dark colors (more on this later) and try to be interviewed in the morning. After a firm handshake, and accepting an invitation to be seated, sit straight and forward (never back) and be spontaneous. Of course, your spontaneity will be born of full intelligence about both the substance and culture of the organization and, to the extent possible, about the person conducting the interview. From this point, you behave out of a kind of educated intuition, warm, charming, succinctly articulate as you appear to be the prototype of the company and the people. And you are these things with a subtle enthusiasm, a refined energy that smacks of the good future of the company. Remember, the first interview is the best; if possible, try not to have a second before you are appointed. You are appointed, now continue on your charismatic course. Remember, you inspire trust and confidence.

- In your work, always be moving toward something.
- Always elevate the conversation.

Power Behavior in the Corporation

Never willingly ennoble anyone in such a way that he may molest you.

—Han Tzu

There is no more miserable human being than one in whom nothing is habitual but indecision.

—William James

What is said when drunk has been thought out beforehand.
—Flemish Proverb

She gave herself, he took her: the third party was time, who made cuckolds of them both.

—Malcolm de Chazal

Go about your work with a calm air of assurance and confidence. The workplace is not the proper forum to express confusion. Never share your major doubts or troubles with anyone with whom you work—your boss, your associates, or your employees. Conversely you will be greatly appreciated if you can share their stress, empathize with their problems, but not intrude into their affairs. Encourage them to greater heights as you celebrate their achievements.

Carefully Maintain Your Social Distance in the Corporation

Surely you must know by now that to move up you must be more concerned with results than with being liked or immediately recognized. It is only natural for the newly appointed to want to be included in the "in" group, and the tendency is to err on the side of forced familiarity. Don't obey this impulse or you will remain in that first echelon group forever. Be sincere, warm, and friendly, but not overly available. If you're going to play on the office softball team and you are a good player, that's O.K. Just don't go out for drinks afterward; or if you do, stay for one drink and be off.

The same is true for other social activities in the office. Even after much experience you may be tempted. But please, please keep social activities in the work place to a minimum. Familiarity may induce some fleeting affection, but it most surely makes you unnecessarily vulnerable and creates a potential for less appreciation. Social intimacy reduces your charismatic and legitimate power potential. It also diminishes your ability to use all of the other power forms (reward, expert, and coercive).

When you are invited to office parties and other social functions, go, but don't stay long. Whatever you do, be warm, be friendly, but stay remote. Keep some mystery about you. Don't encourage others to classify you as ordinary. As new leaders are chosen, the ordinary are eliminated. One of the candidates may be you, and not necessarily because you are so much more brilliant than others. You may be chosen because there is that interesting undefinable quality about you that inspires confidence and performance. When you become the boss, don't encourage parties, birthday celebrations, or any unstructured group activity that promotes informal relationships. What your people need is a highly structured situation in which roles are reinforced and mutual regard is evident. Nothing else will work as well. Regardless of the setting, you must always manifest that special quality and it doesn't come easily in unorganized social events.

Close Personal Relationships in Business Are Rare

Whatever you may have been lead to believe, most business and professional relationships should be limited and those of some depth will be the most fragile you have. Business relationships—in either the profit and non-profit sector—are rooted in production and performance. The warmest, most convivial relationship can turn sour when failures occur. If you don't expect too much in these relationships, you will not be disappointed. The few relationships that endure the test of your bad times will be as precious as they are rare, and treat them so.

When you give yourself in true friendship to a business associate then, in the best Aristotelian sense, you are ultimately more obligated to the friendship than to the company. This is desirable because among the greatest rewards of life will be your true friends. But you should be highly discriminating and not expect many to qualify for these unique relationships.

Never resort to subterfuge, deceit, petty cruelty, hypocrisy, or insincerity. They are the antitheses of the person of power. Keep enough of yourself to yourself that there is always about you some mystery, some mystique, something that prompts this kind of statement: "Yes, I don't really know him, yet I trust him absolutely and I would follow him through the gates of Hell." You don't lie or even shade the truth for any reason. Rather you learn simply to keep your mouth shut during personal moments—at cocktail parties, over coffee, after the athletic outing, and during the warm-ups that always precede a business conversation. Those situations beg for self-revelation. Let the other person talk. Don't be afraid of the pregnant pause. Ask questions and listen well. Incidentally, it is not enough that you practice silence and comment only when the situation invites it. Keep in mind also that people will judge you by what you allow to be said to you; do not listen long to malicious gossip or disloyalty to the company or the supervisors.

Distance Is Absolutely Essential with Subordinates

People who report to you will admire you as much for your social distance as for your professional competence. Even though you are unsure of yourself in your new position, you are expected to radiate confidence, provide inspiration, and to absorb the stress of others. You celebrate their successes, and up to the point of their discharge or reassignment, ease any unnecessary pain and disappointment within your power. You are their leader or potential leader and you cannot do this while being just like everyone else. Do not encourage or attend office luncheons, unless given for special occasions. However, every now and then, take the office staff out to lunch as a group. They will love you for it. Downplay other social functions within the organization unless unusual circumstances dictate your presence. Of course, attend ceremonies, retirements, funerals; they are entirely different because they express respect and concern for co-workers. In these cases, your attendance is essential. You are the leader. Intimacy breeds conflict in the mind of the employee. If you have been promoted from within the organization, your longtime associates will go to great lengths to keep you in the group. Separate yourself from the old group gently. It only hurts a little at first. Do it and you will not only generate respect, but in time your former peers will like you more. In time, both you and they will see the value in your action. The choice facing you in these situations is being liked for maintaining the status quo or being highly regarded. Since you can't have both, don't make the mistake of needing to be liked more than being respected. Command their respect and affection will follow. Effective leadership and extraordinary personal power are impossible the other way around.

Resist Close Personal Relationships with Corporate Peers

Those inclined to test the validity of this truism receive a painful reminder for their efforts. Your close friends should come from *outside* your company. This will be difficult because of your need for reassurance and fellowship. But if you can remain both aloof and likable, you will be the first of your peers to move up. It is even more important to avoid intimate personal relationships with members of the opposite sex. When tempted, bear in mind that such experiences may be fun and a pleasant diversion. But you run the risk of serious involvement and invariably you become more debatable and less respected. Try to reserve your full self for your family and a few close friends from outside the office. To violate your professional composure in the name of self-indulgence is a sure sign of weakness. A last warning: the individual who believes he can keep an office romance a secret from the observant eyes around him is simple minded as well as self-indulgent.

Do Establish Personal Relationships with Those Above You

Contrary to the social distance with employees, and peers, short of sex, try to establish the most intimate relationship possible with those above you. Because of their success, most of them will share inside information gladly and expect some adulation from rising talents. Their good opinion and guidance are essential to your future. Most successful top executives had the benefit of one or more mentoring relationships on the way up. Don't be obsequious or overly flattering in relating to them. To the extent possible, be where they are so they may come to know you personally and be impressed by the achievements of a rising star with an impressive record. Remember, productivity, self-discipline, and charm, plus a little aura of mystery complete the formula from your side.

Dissidents Will Drag You Down

Be careful of informers and dissidents. These are negative individuals who will attempt to get you involved in their cause and grievances. Listen to them only briefly. Although there may be some truth in what they say, they thrive on gossip and pessimism and they can easily include you in their network. Don't shun them completely. In fact, use them to spell out carefully a more positive and progressive attitude. Just be sure they say the right things about you. They are the ones who think they know everything and everyone, and find nothing and few to their liking. They've usually been with the company a long time and have been promoted slowly if at all. They can give you countless reasons for *not* doing something. They are the ones who will always speak critically of your superiors and your associates. They never have a good word for a former employer. Do your best not to socialize with them. Everyone knows what they are and how they operate. They invariably create a conflict within the company and then use their "friends" as sandbags to protect themselves.

The Zealot Is Dangerous to All

Zealotry is a form of irrational protest. It is without substance or sanity, and therefore dangerous. But it can be, at least momentarily charismatic, and ordinarily sensible people can rally around the zealot. They are particularly attractive to the people who have a real or perceived complaint and to those who are habitually lazy and feel entitled to a handout. If you become zealous about anything you should question both your judgment and your motive. You will fail eventually.

Zealousness is invariably excessive and transient. At best, zealots will momentarily create a diversion and then pass into ignominy. Bitter, miserable, and unhappy individuals are left in their path.

All companies, be they business, religious, political, or educational, have their share of zealots, so be forewarned. They are the peculiar ones with glassy-eyed stares obsessed with a personal cause. They are always a bit odd, distant, and distracted. When they engage in a "conversation" with you, their responses indicate they do not listen to anything except for approval of their egocentric cause. They often appear calm and quite collected, but when opportunity arises, they will do almost anything to gain their goal, including slander. Don't laugh at them or discount their fanatic determination. Just do your best to stay distinct from them psychologically, philosophically, and physically.

Do not in any manner support such extremists. They are not rational and will not in any way be persuaded by your own charisma or expertise. Your logic and charm will only make them more hostile toward you. And they can do you considerable damage.

The best way to handle unrelenting zealots is to ignore them. Let them run their course and go their way. Don't respond strongly, whatever the temptation. You'll only provide more ammunition. Keep your composure and your distance. But if this course fails or is impractical, delegate responsibility for direct confrontation as far down your corporate order as possible. The idea is to keep you away from direct confrontation. Your job is to protect your delegate and continue on a charismatic course.

Religion and politics are the social institutions where one is most likely to find zealotry. But all social institutions, formal and informal, have their zealots. In religion and politics you are more apt to find them along the fringes (the far right and the far left) and among the converts. But there are zealots of the latest fads, i.e., technology, TQM, etc. Be careful with them, for they exert an intense though usually short-lived influence.

Drinking and Business Are Totally Incompatible

For you, rarely is it appropriate to mix drinking with business. Drinking always diminishes charisma and expertise. I was out one evening at dinner with a respected business associate, who turned loud and drunken. I never viewed him the same way again. While you may attend the "martini" luncheon, cocktail reception, and dinner party, rarely, if ever, drink anything stronger than tonic water, soda, or cola. Don't make a show of this however. Indeed, try not to be noticed as a nondrinker. You'll make the drinker uncomfortable. Remember any amount of alcohol depresses brain function. Either don't drink at all or save it for non-business. Moderate drinking should only be done with your closest confidants, where business will not be an important consideration.

Attitude to Approach the Seemingly Unattainable

A winning attitude should accompany an organized program implemented with hard work, whether the focus is a job, a love object, affection, or respect. Resistance arises if you press too hard. Be present but don't be pushy. Be available but only for meaningful occasions, which means not too available. Mystique and patience are

> ### "General" Debby
>
> Debby Hopkins, CEO of Lucent, is described as "a relentlessly executing, no-holds-barred, take-no-prisoners, be-in-front-with-the- shield-and-sword, go-to-war, stay-in-the-ditches" leader. A turn-around specialist, without an MBA, she has proven her brilliance at Ford, Unisys, GM Europe, and Boeing. She is almost pathologically committed to doing more than expected.

important words to you. Single-mindedness means you're in the race but wearing blinders. Never be overly specific about your goals. Just pursue them, but remain flexible to others' pursuits by showing self-restraint. Don't say to your close work associate, or best friend, "I have simply got to have that promotion," or "I must have her." And don't reveal such things to those who will finally decide the issue. Let your determination and focus be inferred, not stated, in terms that could later come back to haunt you. Just pursue your set goals and be productive and appropriately ambitious. Smile to cap off your upbeat manner while maintaining a certain remoteness, and you'll win.

Smile

Few gestures can gain as much for the leader as a warm, ready, and genuine smile. It communicates much. It tells people you appreciate them, that you care about them, that they make you feel better, and that you respect them. A smile says thank you, good job, so many things—all good. So many things and you haven't said a word, just a smile. For some reason smiles don't come easily to many people in the business setting. All the better for you. Life is sufficiently serious that we need not be

> **Smile**
>
> My father always wore a smile and called strangers "neighbor." When he died, I found this sign on his refrigerator door, "One day I met a man without a smile. I gave him one." Today, I have that sign in my study where I can see it everyday.

serious all the time. The leader who maintains distance as he or she engages in warmth and sometimes laughter is most admired and effective.

On Being Recognized

You may feel the need to be recognized for your initial accomplishments. You may reconcile yourself to what appears to be the status quo, or you may go to your boss and diplomatically ask "Why? I'm doing all these things, and you haven't noticed." Don't think and certainly never say, "It's not fair." Let your results speak for themselves. It is best for you to remain silent. In doing so, you neither present yourself as dangerously ambitious or so immature and lacking in self-confidence that you can only produce when you are constantly praised. In time, you will be recognized.

Don't Undercut Your Competition

Don't allow ambition to lead you into undercutting your professional peers in conversation with colleagues or superiors, or in business transactions. Discrediting another is a device of the inadequate and the insecure. You must comport yourself with propriety and principle as well as being productive, for as front runner you will invite faultfinding by your fellows—both competitors and friends. There is simply no acceptable reason for denigrating a professional associate. You cannot build a successful career on the bodies of your professional competition. Let them talk about you, and they will if you remain quiet. Your task is to ensure that their critical review yields nothing really questionable about your professional behavior. Remember, what you say in casual conversation counts as much as what you say in business or professional meetings. Indeed, casual comments are more telling than those delivered from the podium.

You Needn't Alienate Others to Bring Change

When the time comes to take exception to a proposed corporate policy or practice, and this will sometimes be the case, take exception to the idea or the issue itself but not to the person who disagrees with you. The individual who thoughtfully develops an alternate plan and advocates it strongly deserves respect. Spend as much time thinking about how you are going to achieve your goal as you have in determining what the goal should be. Be careful that you respectfully acknowledge your ideological adversaries as you pursue your goal. Do this in word, deed, and spirit. There should be only temporary differences between you. When you have won your case, or the larger measure of it, take the time to reinforce a good relationship with the loser. Because of your success, you will have corporate enemies. Some unpopular people help you when they are your enemy and attack you personally. But you must not develop a reputation for being inconsiderate or having a disregard for the worth of others. Speak to the issues and don't personalize comments. Be a graceful and generous winner and you'll keep excellent relations with those who differ with you in principle but who never doubt your motives in acting as you do.

Sex in the Office Is Always Inappropriate

It is inevitable that opportunities for contact with the opposite sex present themselves. Sexual offers arise in direct proportion to the success of the individual. Sexual intimacy in corporate life is fraught with peril. Users often discover they are being used. The repercussions can be immense, both professionally and personally. When these compromises of position occur, they inevitably jeopardize the effectiveness and the future of the leader. But you must make a choice: Is it worth the gamble? Remember, you will pay a price and it could be a steep one in terms of your career, not to mention the permanent personal consequences. Look at Jesse Jackson, Morrison Kaudson, and Mary Cunningham. It even finally caught up with Bill Clinton.

This is not to suggest that friendships are not desirable and important to all of us or that friendships between members of the opposite sex cannot greatly enrich our lives. However, in a corporate settings they rarely lead to happy marriages. Both close friendship and marriage in the corporation make the leader less effective, even though there are legitimate relationships. Inappropriate sexual relationships can tarnish the leader's image to a degree he or she can neither regain former luster nor remove the stain.

Try to reserve your close friendships in the business for very special people. But remember that a night on the town

Sex in the Office

The very admired and successful President of Hillsdale College was exposed after a long affair with his assistant who was also his daughter-in-law. Under his leadership, Hillsdale had achieved a unique national niche and had been able to attract supporters like William Bennett, Henry Kissinger and Bob Lutz of Chrysler and Oxide. His long-standing behavior was finally exposed and he crawled off to oblivion.

with an employee can ultimately be as compromising as going to bed with one. Unless you are of extraordinary character or you have a tested nonsexual relationship, avoid such situations as cocktails after work, intimate suppers, one-on-one dinners, or any situation that can lead to intimacy. If the temptation is irresistible, consider seeking professional guidance just as you would any potentially dysfunctional behavior.

Sexual relations with co-workers invariably lead to a great variety of problems. The person often becomes overly protective of you or begins to expect special advantages. Your exhibition of personal self-indulgence, in time, reduces your effective use of each of the other power forms (legitimate, expert, reward, and coercive). Unless you are an absolute monarch, don't think you will be exempt from the sanctions. Play around in the office, but not that way.

On the other hand, so long as you aren't guilty of anything, some rumors and gossip about your sexual attractiveness enhance personal charisma. It's always good for you to give them something to speculate on. Just don't make it possible for anyone to cite grounds for suspicion, because if they can, they will.

Finally, sexual relations with your boss can hurt you for the same reasons you shouldn't have such relationships with persons who work for you. There are compelling reasons why you should not do this: social convention, discovery from the wrong quarter, but mostly your own mental health. In time, the impact on your own self-esteem will be damaging. Intimacy for personal advantage can lead to a corruption of self that affects all-important relationships in your life. You cannot conceal this behavior from others, for office personnel will be quick to detect unusual closeness. Sexual relationships that occur inappropriately do not arise for no reason. They always denote a search for elements missing in a person's life. They provide short-term gratification with long-term complications. They are, therefore, an ineffective answer to a deeper problem. Professional help is an intelligent approach for any unrestrained or immoderate behavior. And sexual intimacy without genuine affection can cheapen the experience to the point that the real poetry is lost (at least for you). But in the short run, and for some in the long run, sexual intimacy with your superior can provide a distinct power advantage. If you want to play this dangerous game go ahead, if your boss is dumb enough. But you are likely to lose.

Be Happy: High Intelligence and Great Power Rarely Go Together

If you scored high on standardized tests and were a most successful student you must approach leadership roles carefully. Although there is some evidence that intelligence, as measured by tests, relates to first-level executive effectiveness, *there is no established relationship between high intelligence and higher-level executive success*. This doesn't mean that there is a negative relationship between leadership and intelligence. It does mean, however, that high intelligence doesn't appear to be a distinct advantage for the aspiring leader. Among the brilliant, the difference is one of perception and patience. The very intelligent person tends to perceive more quickly and is inclined to become impatient or even condescending with others who may be no less competent. In this exchange, they eventually distance themselves from those they are expected to lead. Their followers or subordinates grudgingly respect them but rarely admire them. Thus they are unable to lead. The brilliant find it difficult to speak for "their" people. They are wrong so many times they finally don't even try.

If you are exceptionally bright and well educated, keep this in mind as you progress up the corporate ladder. Keep (or get) the common touch. But remember, just a touch. You can make it, although your I.Q. is no guarantee. Just pay as much attention to your productivity, to the image you project, and to the methods you use, for you will receive no special indulgences. It's fine to be a speed reader or exceptional in any way, but the less said about your brilliance, the better.

- Never take exception to individuals, only issues.
- To the extent possible, establish intimate non-sexual relationships with people at the highest corporate levels.
- A person who isn't ego invested, won't work when you're not watching.

- Power often is more perception and comportment than authority or means.
- Don't engage in extensive intelligence activities; they can become an abusive preoccupation and prevent production.
- The answer to winning is often not playing.
- Don't ask for recognition, but expect it.
- At office parties, come early and leave early.
- With subordinates, respect and trust are more important than friendship.
- Rock the boat, but get along with people.

Complements to Power

It is only shallow people who do not judge by appearance.
—Oscar Wilde

People care more about being thought to have taste than about being either good, clever, or amiable.
—Samuel Butler (II)

"**D**arling, it's not how you feel but how you look that counts. And you look marvelous!" These words from Fernando Lamas are more than funny, because how you look and present yourself not only significantly influences others but effects how you feel. *This chapter includes recommendations on subjects often judged superficial and either disdained or left unconsidered in books on personal achievement and success, but they are important to you.* So let's consider clothing, automobiles, office furnishings, service clubs, and spouses. Such accoutrements become accepted over the years as marks of status, authority and power. While these appointments are fairly standard, there are subcultures in the United States and abroad in which certain styles or models denote local insignia of sophistication and power. "Proceed carefully" in adapting to these variations until you are thoroughly familiar with regional nuances. Dress for the special province if you wish, but these recommendations are formulated to make certain that you are "in" in most of the subcultures that you will inhabit. They are de rigueur throughout the United States and most of the rest of the world.

What You Wear Is a Power Statement

If we are what we think, we are also what we wear. You can enhance both your legitimate power and you self-esteem with clothing. How you dress can tell much more about you than what you say or the information in your professional resume. It often has as much to do with your promotions as with your professional accomplishments. With few exceptions, provincial aristocracies and senior executives dress much the same all over the country and most of the world, for that matter. These individuals can spot a kindred soul anywhere. I loved this line from Sherlock Holmes to Dr. Watson about clothing and appearance, "You did not know where to look, and so you missed all that was important. I can never bring you to realize the importance of sleeves, the suggestiveness of thumbnails, or the great issue that may hang from a (shoe) lace."

Unless you are the son or daughter of the chairman of the board or you just don't give a damn (or you are already the chairman of the board), you should choose tasteful but conservative clothing. Refinement, not flash, is your taste in clothing. Although there are a number of good conservative clothing stores in each section of the country, the only universally acceptable store in the United States has been Brooks Brothers and, in recent years, even Brooks Brothers has made compromises into more casual clothing. There are also Burberry's, Polo, Nordstrom, Saks, Neiman Marcus, and Britches, but be careful of any trendy fashions and extremes in style. And extremes do not suit you. If you cannot now afford these stores, go in and look carefully so that you can find a less expensive version in another store. Joseph A. Banks is a good less expensive substitute and most communities have at least one good, locally owned clothing store. And, of course, these stores also have women's divisions, and regardless of what follows, I do not presume to approach women's clothing with authority although the same general message applies to both women and men.

As noted above, today Brooks Brothers also makes mistakes. Perhaps they were influenced by the success of Paul Stewart's more stylish clothing. They now offer some variety in styles.

Resist the vicissitudes of fashion even when an ordinarily reliable source tries to persuade you otherwise. Let me be more specific. For men the timeless *three-button* "sack" suit is classic. You can't go wrong here. However, today you can get by in a two-button, but try to find the *three-button*. Sadly, many stores have compromised, but if you press their sales people, they can usually find what you want. Your trousers should always be cuffed, unless you wear cowboy boots. A double-breasted suit is acceptable when you want to push conservative to the edge, but never wear a button-down shirt with your double-breasted suit. At the very least, you should have a blue chalk, dark blue or black pinstripe, a gray pinstripe, and a navy blue suit. A charcoal gray suit is also appropriate.

After Six

I had been invited to Texas to deliver an "inspiring" address to the top 25 benefactors of a major university.

I dressed in a tan Palm Beach suit, wore a blue oxford cloth shirt, and wing-tip cordovan shoes. Now years before, my mother had taught me that after six a man should wear a dark suit, white shirt, and black shoes, but I thought that that was passe today and besides this was not Washington, DC, it was sunny southern Texas.

When the university president and the chairman of the board picked me up at the hotel they were both wearing dark suits, white shirts, and black shoes. After a few pleasantries, they drove me to a lovely house on the Gulf (I still remember some original French Impressionist paintings there). I was met by the host and hostess, he was wearing a dark suit, white shirt, and black shoes. During cocktails I met twenty-three other men in dark suits, white shirts, and black shoes.

Today, I always think of that evening and my Mother's advice as I dress for a dinner meeting.

A man's warm weather wardrobe might include lighter shades, tan or light blue, some seer sucker pinstripes, all of precisely the same cut. Keep in mind that dark colors convey authority. Don't go to an important professional meeting wearing light colors, particularly with corporate superiors or with strangers. Cultivate the practice of wearing a lapel handkerchief—white cotton with only a point (or two) of white showing. Never use silk, satin, or nonwhite handkerchiefs except with a tuxedo. Although junior executives rarely wear sportcoats to work, these should also be *three-button* and conservative—navy blue, camel, and most tweeds. Coordinating trousers should be cuffed. (No proper gentlemen would wear anything else.)

From time to time during your life, you will be tempted by current fads and trends. Note the current dress revolution but don't succumb completely, even if your company has "dress-down" days. Stay preppy. Newspapers like *The New York Times* and *The Washington Post* are taken in by the caprices of fashions and at times recommend different styling in suits or stores that promote styles that are antithetical to the power seeker. Custom tailoring in your exact specifications is acceptable. Although expensive, having a suit from Saville Row in London or Hong Kong and a half-dozen shirts from Pec and Company in New York adds a tasteful flourish to your wardrobe.

Men's shirts should be predominantly white cotton, some with quiet stripes, with an occasional oxford blue. Collars should be straight or button-down, but always cotton. They should be "standard" with no full spread or round collars. And no tie pins. Get 100 percent cotton—no polyester, wash and wear, or combinations. Be sure they are laundered and pressed well each time and if you can't do the job, send them out after one wearing with a request to be

Dress Right, Dress Left

A perfect public example of point, counter-point dress is the contrast between George W. Bush and Bill Clinton. Note virtually everything about Bill Clinton's dress is inappropriate: his tie is a half-windsor, his shirt collar is too wide and starched, and his suits are all two button. On the other hand, George W's tie is fore-in-hand with a dimple, his collar is soft cotton either straight or button-down, and his suits and sport coats are both three and two button. Of course, both of them made it to the U.S. Presidency; you decide the difference between the two. For purposes of dispassionate comparison, note that John F. Kennedy dressed almost exactly like George W. Bush.

"boxed and little or no starch." Discreet monograms are a nice touch when on your left sleeve cuff (3/8" up) and not on your shirt pocket. You can compromise the whole outfit by the wrong shirt or the monogram in the wrong place.

The same is true for men's ties, socks, and shoes. Silk rep (striped) ties are always acceptable as are foulards. For anything else, ask an experienced salesperson, but remember even experienced salespersons often sell you what you like rather than what you need. For business, you should forego club, paisley, or plaid ties. Tie your tie in a fore-in-hand knot, never a Windsor or a half-Windsor. Bow ties are worn by men who are a bit to the left or right of center, but never too

> **Breaking the Rules**
>
> A friend of mine who had "arrived" in his profession following the classic rules of charm and dress began to affect peculiarities. He started driving a pick-up truck, he wore red socks with a tuxedo, when he wore socks at all, but he always tied a fore-in-hand knot in his tie, wore soft cotton shirts, blue sport coat and khaki trousers. He broke the rules, but he continued to convey a knowing message.

far, they usually equivocate. My advice: don't wear them. Your first pair of dress shoes should be black and then dark brown. They should be low-heeled, lace oxfords, not loafers. Good quality moccasins are acceptable. Never buy Italian or French, whatever your girlfriend says. Your hosiery should be calf-length in only two colors, black or dark blue.

Don't wear jewelry except for a thin watch and a modest wedding band. Stay away from bracelets, neck chains, or gaudy rings and watches. Diamond rings are not in for men, regardless of how much they cost.

A man's tuxedo should be completely black shawl or peak (not notch) collar. Shawl collars are the most classic, but both are acceptable. Plaid or fancy jackets mark you as both immature and unsophisticated except at Christmas parties, etc. You should also have a very simple white dinner jacket. Your accessories should be conservative-plain and simple. Keep on hand a white, non-frilly shirt with studs and matching cuff links and a tie-it-yourself black bow tie and no wing collar. And *don't* wear the Hollywood trends (colored shirt, no tie, fore-in-hand tie, etc.). And until you are knighted, wear a black cummerbund, no vest. You might want to wear a satin or cotton handkerchief in your lapel pocket with only a touch of white showing. Your shoes should be plain patent leather black oxfords, either pumps or slippers. You could get away with other black shoes as long as they are not wingtips.

Women's business clothing should be classic but not dowdy. No one will say "lose your femininity" but stay away from low-cut blouses or sweaters, skirts slit to there, and anything too tight. Don't, however, feel that you have to fade into the boardroom woodwork. Develop your own style. Get the help of a fashion consultant. Most top stores like Saks have them these days. Read fashion monthlies to keep up with the styles. Most such publications these days cater to the career woman and offer helpful tips on dressing for success. Beware of pastel colors except in obviously social situations and don't be afraid to wear red.

Women should follow the same rules as men in looking for simplicity of clothing design, natural fabrics, and uncomplicated jewelry. Colors for women should be essentially the same as those recommended for men. If your leadership role takes you on frequent trips, make sure you buy skirts, tops, and jackets that work well together. Keep the heels medium—spikes can rob you of the dignity you require. I am advised that if you must wear offbeat shoes, make sure they are Walter Steiger's, Manola Blanik, or Maud Frizon or at least look like them; most women can afford Etienne Aigner. Stay away from brightly colored hosiery for daytime. At night, you might try sparkly ones, if they're silk. A simple black dress is a must—it will take you anywhere well. A St. John suit will say all there is to say and because you probably cannot afford a St. John, buy a more modestly priced look-a-like.

A conservative approach to your hair and makeup is always better. Remember less is best. Mascara, eye shadows and eyeliners applied in double or triple doses is a sign of spending too much time with cosmetics. The same holds true for extra long nails. As for today's body piercings and tatoos, never! Cologne is great...but not in extra heavy doses. Oh, and never pull out a compact mirror to check your hair or makeup in a meeting...it is rude and distracting.

Dress this way and you will have the tacit acceptance

Mascara

During the 2000 election controversy, the Florida Secretary of State, Katherine Harris, played an important role and catapulted to national attention. Her statements were for the most part, thoughtful and fair, but her mascara clouded her presentation and made consideration of her points more difficult.

of your corporate power hierarchy, even those who don't completely conform. You will be counted quietly as a knowing brother or sister.

Cars Imply Power

Your transportation should be as conservative, tasteful, and "aware" as your clothing to convey the same kind of power message. For the rising executive, it's better to drive a used BMW or Mercedes than a new Ford. The power elite may drive anything they wish, but most drive (if they drive at all) Mercedes, Range Rover, Jaguar, BMW, Lexus, Cadillac, Chrysler or Lincoln. Occasionally, they may add very expensive foreign cars to the list. The Swedish Volvo and SAAB are often choices of members of the liberal establishment. And those who really understand the subtleties of car choice will tell you, "One doesn't drive a Cadillac: one is driven."

Understated Jeeps, Land Rovers, and Broncos, or even American-built pickup trucks are driven by some as fun cars. But never drive a Jeep or a pickup truck that is two-toned or has anything painted on the sides—words or stripes. Make your choice a solid color with *no* ornamentation.

Other than the luxury models listed above, there are modestly appointed models of Ford, Chevrolet, and Plymouth. Never buy a fancy looking car of any kind. Don't put wire wheels on anything and don't get personalized license plates. Forget motorcycles until you have arrived. And don't even think about American cars like Corvettes, Trans Ams, or Cameros. If you do drive one, keep it parked around the corner and removed from your office. Whatever kind you drive, keep it clean and neat.

Remember your car is a power accessory. If you've read this far, you can estimate a car's power quotient for yourself. Bear in mind that if you get the wrong color, design, or accessories, you can alter the impact dramatically. Any model smacks of taste and more power if it is solid black, dark green, dark blue, maroon or dark gray. And don't put on bumper stickers or decals on anything but pickup trucks, Jeeps, station wagons, and SUVs.

There are some ultra expensive custom makes like Ferrari, Maserati, Aston Martin, and Lotus, all of which bespeak affluence. But they convey more of the capricious eccentric, the flamboyant entrepreneur, or even the spoiled and self-indulgent rich than they do of the authentic power. You may envy them, but rarely follow them on a serious venture. If you drive a sports car, make it a second or third car. The European are more clearly power statements than the American or Japanese; American automobiles typically are usually too conspicuous and Japanese too efficient. However, for some Americans only American cars will be acceptable, and then not a Cadillac. Top of the line Buicks or perhaps a dark colored Lincoln could be considered.

Finally, cars should also be fun. Your car should make you feel as well as look better. Try to bring yourself to think of automobiles as aesthetic experiences as well as transportation. Approach your motor car as a work of art that will be viewed by your associates as representing you. Select it as such and care for it that way and it can constitute a main element among the accessories of power.

How You Decorate Your Office Can Help Pave the Way

Your office says a great deal about who and what you are. And you are a confident, productive, and caring person who can shoulder the problems and anxieties of others. Your office reflects you. It is your subtle statement of self-confidence, upward mobility, and performance.

Like your dress and automobile, your office should be tasteful and conservative rather than modern and fashionable. It should be impeccable, neat, and subtly personal.

Furniture should be strong and lean to darker shades rather than lighter. And you should never sit behind your desk. Try to arrange your office so that your desk is against a wall or window. Do your best to obtain the highest quality possible. Carpeting and rugs, although hardwood may be better, should be of the same high quality and preferably of a different color from that in the outer work space and other offices. The colors should be as royal and comfortable as possible, and not at all flashy. Seating should be inviting, but not overly plush. Leathers are generally too cold. The look of your office should imply sophistication, refinement, and tradition. The rounded corners and deep colors of the wood grains are more sensuous than certain. Chippendale and Georgian are good power accessories in furniture. Persian and Oriental rugs will always be appropriate. Reserve crown moldings and wainscoting for when you move up the ladder. While it should not obviously be furnished far above your station, it should gently push the upper limits of your present peer group. You are always striving to be the best.

It is tasteful to have a few personal items on display, but don't overwhelm your visitors with your honors, which are best displayed at home in your private study. Pictures of your

family or of you on holidays with good friends will lend a
touch of personal warmth to the impressive area. But unless
you are a medical doctor, dentist, psychologist or lawyer who
might need to reinforce your qualifications, don't hang your
diploma(s) in your office.

Don't cover your walls with photos of yourself with prominent
people. It only tells your visitors who you think are more important than you. Have plants and especially flowers in your office.
They lend a sensitive and caring quality to the occupant. Just don't
go too far for excessive anything conveys too much self-revelation.
Preserve the mystery.

Your shelves should include volumes beyond your particular
professional interest, books and objects that tell something about
you. Your coffee table should include your tasteful personal
favorites (*Harpers, Fortune, Harvard Business Review, Poetry*), as well
as professional journals in your field or related fields. If you are
president, have the American flag and perhaps the flag of your
state or company in your office.

Joining Clubs, Civic Organizations, and Other Groups Requires Judicious Decisions

Be careful in accepting invitations to join any group. Generally
it is better not to join than to accept your first invitations. Do this
and you may later look back and regret it because your decision
has long enduring implications. Unless your company insists otherwise, set your sights on the highest service organization or club
and don't settle for less. Indeed, unless you are in a small town,
consider not accepting membership in any social or business club.
Speak and attend when invited, but unless pressed by your boss,
don't join. So long as you remain productive and charming, not
being a member of the club will add to your aura of mystery and
general attractiveness. Your charisma (social distance) will also
grant more weight to your expertise (expert power).

In addition to the feeling of belonging (almost always over-
valued), too many of us are driven by an almost paranoid feeling of wanting to be accepted by every group possible. We
think that if they accept us, they won't talk about us or we'll be
present when they do.

Resist this trap. It's good for them to talk about you. In fact, it
is infinitely better for them to talk about you, even though at times

their comments may be erroneous and a bit off target. Let them talk. In general it is best to stay away from such informal professional groups. Don't listen to people who say, "You should be seen here or belong to this group." They're talking about themselves and other manager-types, not leaders. Joining service clubs can be just another way for others to know you too well.

It is, however, appropriate and desirable for you to accept social invitations or speaking invitations to almost any organization. Be charming, attentive, and general, but keep moving. They will regard you so much more highly if you remain warmly elusive. Be seen and be heard only where appropriate. Don't, through your own insecurity, be too anxious to become one of the boys or girls. You are going to be their leader.

Your Spouse or Significant Other

The role of spouses or significant others in professional activities often looms large in high-level positions. From the job interview to retirement, like it or not, your spouse is an extension of you. In so many ways, your professional success can be influenced by your spouse or significant other. Your mate must always, female or male, translate his or her behavior in terms of your best interest. If you are both professionals, simply reverse roles depending on circumstance. An unhappy spouse can affect performance at work, your job evaluation and whether or not a position or promotion is offered. Domineering partners can make a mockery of your power and authority. A spouse can be a social embarrassment by word, dress, drink, or manners. There is the clinging spouse, the brooding spouse, the sexy spouse, the talking spouse, the opinionated spouse, the tipsy spouse, etc.

If your mate is involved in your work, you both have to consider how your spouse is affected by the power structure demanded at work that may be totally different from that at home. Even if you use your partner to critique your performance, complete candor can be difficult, and some relationships have been strained to the breaking point. Handle this with care, but if your spouse is inclined, share all. Remember, finally, there are no secrets.

Although there are exceptions, it may be better that your spouse not be directly involved in your work. If you have one of those rare relationships where you both feel your spouse can help you in your work, establish clear limits that you both understand, and that your employees understand. Your spouse should not in any way be involved in business discussion where the power/authority structure may be compromised. This will be difficult, but insist upon it. Even if you feel comfortable with it, your business associates should be informed and the special needs explained to be certain they do not feel intimidated or demoralized by an unaccountable spouse stepping into positions of delegated authority. Remember Abigail Adams, Edith Wilson, and Hilary Clinton in the White House.

Assuming that your spouse is involved in your professional life, then the spouse must be pleasantly subordinate in *all* professional settings, including those that appear to be ostensibly social. While the spouse is due respect, you must have deference of position. How many spouses have you heard making denigrating comments about a mate or seen pouting because of inattention in the corner of the country club ballroom.

There has been an unfortunate practice in some organizations attempting to elevate the role of the spouse. Some are even being assigned secretarial and personal assistant roles. Be very thoughtful about this prospect for the practice may make for more marital pressures and less charismatic potential for you. Exercised poorly, it can also reduce significantly each of your other power forms (expert, legitimate, reward, and coercive).

In Sum

Finally, remember that all of these complements, even exercised by a virtuoso, will not amount to anything in your upward mobility without production born of extraordinary self-discipline. These complements can significantly help you gain admission to the club of the diffident. They will make you more acceptable but they are not substitutes for hard work.

- Always wear dark colors where you want to be important.
- Dress, at least a little, like the provincial aristocracy.
- No fur, no leather.
- If your spouse is going to be involved, it should be in a cameo role.
- Strong women don't have to sacrifice femininity.
- Happy people always remember their roots.

Power and Communication in the Corporation

We often refuse to accept an idea merely because the tone of voice in which it has been expressed is unsympathetic to us.
—Friedrich Nietzsche

Silence is the unbearable repartee.
—G. K. Chesterton

The language of excitement is at best picturesque merely. You must be calm before you can utter oracles.
—Henry David Thoreau

One's eyes are what one is; one's mouth, what one becomes.
—John Galsworthy

If I have said something to hurt a man once, I shall not get the better of this by saying many things to please him.
—Dr. Samuel Johnson

The secret of the demagogue is to make himself as stupid as his audience so that they believe they are as clever as he.
—Karl Kraus

To give reason for anything is to breed a doubt of it.
—William Hazlitt

To move into real power positions, you must know how to speak and write the English language. Most recent college graduates do not. So much for education today.

Your grammar should be impeccable, for your use of the language will be more important than your vocabulary. Don't split infinitives and end sentences with prepositions, or use the wrong verb form. Avoid fad terms like "marvelous," "bottom-line," "matrix management," "host," "impact" (as a verb) or too many colloquialisms from your youth ("My ole daddy used to say..."). Don't use the lazy or uneducated language that characterize so many: "ok," "you know," "anyways," "eh," "Do you know what I mean?" And don't use any word, phrase or expression too often: "super," "great," "later" (for goodbye). It simply marks you as less educated and unimaginative. The key to good expression is simple straightforward English used correctly, from time to time arranged in an unusual, even dramatic way.

Discipline is required here as in all things. It is acceptable to use less familiar words occasionally like "arcane," "anomaly," "obviate," and "dichotomize." It makes people think you're intelligent, but don't use such words more than once in a presentation. And don't use them twice before the same group or individual.

In writing and speaking, be clear, brief, bold, and poetic. Then be silent. Be able to do this with words. Instead of saying, "Jerry Ford wasn't heard of much after he left office," try, "His last day in office, Jerry Ford got on an airplane and flew out of national awareness." If you don't think you can do this, at least a little, get yourself a good college grammar book and start your lessons from page 1. Subscribe to *Poetry* by writing to 601 S. Morgan St., P.O. Box 4348, Chicago, IL 60680. Your efforts will pay big dividends all the rest of your life. And don't start using a word finder or a thesaurus until you've mastered the basic grammar book.

Reading and rereading poetry, literature, and history will prove helpful for you. They inspire you, provide examples for your work, and suggest to others a breadth to your sophistication.

The Effective Public Speaker Wins the Crown

A speech is a superb opportunity to use the sources or power and you must cultivate the skill. Public speaking is one of the easiest but most feared things we do. There are courses available, but if you choose this route, don't tell anyone in the office. They may think you're too ambitious and threatening. The best way to learn to speak is to speak. The two most natural fears we have are falling and public speaking. Anyone of reasonable motivation can learn to be an excellent public speaker. Just do it as often as you can, and remember the ingredients mentioned earlier: clarity, briefness, bold-

The Great Communicator

Ronald Reagan was known as the "great communicator." When he spoke, his physical presence was always dignified without pomposity. His language was simple and succinct, his humor was self-denigrating and his speeches were bold and direct. It was as if he was speaking our thoughts. And he wrote his own speeches.

ness, and poetry. In speaking, add in a strong spirit of enthusiasm and sincerity. Remember that giving information is not the prime purpose of your presentation. Whether you are giving a 25 minute speech or a two minute television interview, you want to leave the audience with these perceptions: authority, confidence, warmth, and humor.

Always be sure your subject is worthwhile, which means that it may be somewhat controversial and call for risk taking on your part. This is the boldness part. If you are not going to say something, don't speak. In each presentation, repeat your primary message at least three times: tell them what you are going to tell them, tell them, and then tell them what you've told them. And do it all in less than 30 minutes. Try to start your speech with a humorous note, but don't tell prepared stories. From time to time during your remarks, if humor seems appropriate to this particular audience, go ahead. Start at a softer speaking level and gradually increase your volume. Regardless of what you are saying, your audience will think your speech is getting better and better. And speak more quickly than more slowly. It will keep you from using too many um's and uh's and will force people to the edges of their seats to get your astute and electrifying message.

In every speech, your facial expression is important. "Happy and reassuring" wins and "fearful-evasive or angry-threatening" loses. The happy, reassuring look is one with raised eyebrows, teeth showing, and head tilted upward. Give your appearance the strong and happy look.

As in writing, always try to look for better ways to say the same thing. Many have found that reading and writing poetry help. You may speak from notes, but generally it is best to write out your speech and learn to deliver a prepared text through practice. It will let your audience know that you are serious about the assignment. It will also be more impressive. And if you learn to do it right (practice), you will win every audience you address. After this reading, should you still choose notes over a script, write out your full text anyway. Then make notes from your already written text.

You can give a great speech from notes, and occasionally extemporaneously. But both techniques can also be disastrous if you happen to be a touch off in your timing or your enthusiasm. If you know how to deliver a speech from a text, you'll give some great speeches and occasionally you may be as good, but you'll *never* have a loser. End your presentation on a lofty, inspiring, and grateful note, and try to make it appear spontaneous. Do these things and you'll be in the same league with Winston Churchill, Abba Eban, and John F. Kennedy, or at least close to them. Increasingly, there are more impressive speakers among women who are assuming positions of prominence. The same rules should effect the same good results.

> Winston Churchill was considered by many the greatest speaker of the 20th century. During World War II his speeches inspired his countrymen and, indeed, the entire free world. And Winston Churchill practiced an hour on every five-minute "extemporaneous" speech he ever gave.

The Podium as a Lever

Whenever possible, speak from behind an elevated podium and stand when speaking. When you enter a meeting room, take a center or end seat where you can make eye contact with everyone involved in the meeting. Audio visual aids and power-point presentations can be helpful but can also reduce your personal charisma (the main ingredient in influence). Use them sparingly. Bear in mind the risk, and stay in command. Your personal qualities will deliver the message. People speaking consistently on the same subject find that one day they are eloquent and the next day flat. Don't let this discourage you. It should challenge you to improve.

An elevated podium gives you and your message strength, stature, and importance. Don't be so shy or confident that you don't ask for one. If you can get a couple of flags on either side, so much the better. After you have the rapt attention of your audience, relaxing on a nearby table top or stepping down in front of the podium can be a nice touch. Don't do this however, unless you're sure you have your audience.

Unless you are brilliant, it's best that there are no questions after a speech, and even then, a poor question can spoil an effective presentation. Instead, invite those with questions or comments to come to the front after the session is over. In this way, you provide the opportunity for reaction without threatening your image before the full audience.

On those occasions when you must answer questions, remember that you can still retain control. Don't argue with a strong dissenter. Respond politely but equivocally. If you're asked a question you consider disruptive, remember that you can evade the question and give any answer, however remote, to the question. Then move to the next questioner. Keep your answers reasonably brief and be in a hurry. Try to dust off what you're going to say before opening your mouth. Don't be afraid of long pauses or simple yes or no answers. They are good for effect and also give you time to think. Close the question and answer session using the same method you used to close your speech: Thank them, then end on a lofty, inspiring note.

If You Have a Choice, Speak in the Morning

It's always better to speak in the morning. Both you and your audience are more alert. Dinners are the poorest time to discuss business, be interviewed, or deliver speeches. When you are being interviewed for a position, always try to get the first interview of the day. If you must be a banquet speaker, be especially brief. Be as funny as you can, have no more than one serious thought, and express it succinctly with feeling. Save your really substantive speeches for earlier in the day.

Luncheon speeches are a cross between morning and evening. When you are scheduled for a talk, assuming you've prepared your speech in advance, eat lightly—only fish, fowl, or veal. Go to bed early, read something other than your speech, sleep, have a light breakfast alone and rehearse your speech. Try not to discuss other serious subjects before the event. Don't drink alcohol or eat heavily. Avoiding alcohol before a speech is a must.

One-on-One Speaking Is Always Best

You may be tempted to make a sales call or a presentation in the company of experts or influential associates—don't. You will find that both your case and your good fortune are due to you and you alone. This is true whether you are selling computers or houses, making a presentation to an audience, being considered for promotion, or courting a prospective mate. Whatever you don't know, or think you may need, get it before you go, and leave the others out of the transaction. However, in fund raising, a person of impressive means and station can open doors, but you must make the pitch.

Consider Every Group Business Meeting a Mistake

The exercise of power in groups is a fascinating process, and infinitely more complicated than a relationship of only two. Before considering any kind of professional meeting, remember this: *Consider every group meeting a mistake.* If it is utterly inescapable, so be it. This will force you to remember that most of the time people spend

Meetings to Death

Jane was sales manager for the Ritz Carlton Residences. She loved the sales; indeed, she sold $25 million in two weeks. She enjoyed the people and respected the product but the interminable unplanned meetings invariably dampened her enthusiasm and her respect for her bosses.

in group meetings is wasted and the time you must spend there is of questionable value. Studies indicate that senior executives in "average" companies spend 50 percent of their time in meetings. What a terrible waste.

If you must meet with others, use group time in the most profitable manner. Use expert, reward and especially charismatic power in such meetings. Try to downplay your legitimate, and coercive authority. Should the group accomplish little, you can still try to keep everyone on track. And this will lend to your charismatic image.

In Groups, Wait and Think

The most common error committed in groups by the informed, articulate, efficient, would-be charismatic leader (you), is the tendency to speak too much too soon. Unless you are speaking about group procedure, don't speak until all data are in. Save yourself for later as you listen and organize your thoughts. Then you can make your succinct but detailed observations and recommendations with due consideration for the ideas of all the other major participants in the meeting.

Remember to think before you speak. When you do so, speak with obvious respect for others in the group, but speak with utter confidence. Do not dwell on things about which you are uncertain. If your case isn't strong enough for you to do all of these things, then don't speak at all. Chalk the meeting up as another mistake and learn from the experience. You can never really consider this experience a waste if you learn from every error.

You may find yourself jockeying for position with someone who appears to be your equal. Don't fight for control; just wait. After all, your purpose is to achieve common good and not be threatened by other talent. As often happens, your opponent will lose control and talk too much. Then the day will be yours. You're much more likely to overestimate the skill of an opponent and thus feel pressure. Just be patient and before long the group will look to you for direction.

When you are presiding or are the visiting authority, groups are a different matter. Here you can demonstrate clearly the effective use of power. The key is to speak with enthusiasm and confidence. At the same time, you convey respect for the ideas of each member of the group. From time to time, look at each of them directly as you move along at a steady, no-nonsense pace. Speak your thoughts as if you are speaking to an individual and not to a group. Believe what you're saying or do not say it. Don't relax too much or you may miscue and run the risk of having your meeting degenerate. This is a good reason never to chair a group when you are tired. And this is more likely to be in the late afternoons and evenings.

How to Win in Groups

How do you become really effective in groups? First, understand the group environment. Why does the group exist? What is its goal—both stated and implicit? Since few ask this question, you are already ahead of the game. And you're setting the stage for accomplishment simply by attempting to deal with "Why are we here?"

Most groups exist for two purposes. Ostensibly, people come together as a group to get a particular job done. In business it may be to develop a selling strategy, to save a particularly difficult financial problem, or to plan for an uncertain competitive future. The group is expected to focus on designated tasks. But what do we see? A certain amount of foolishness, horseplay, discussion of weekend activities, and other personal diversions. This is because the group also serves certain social and emotional needs of the participants. Even though it serves purely no business purpose, you must tolerate a modicum of socialization. No matter how effective you are, your group will not be solely task-oriented. In fact, the average group spends about 50 percent of its time meeting social and emotional needs. Little wonder meetings should be approached with trepidation.

But with your ability, the group can usually accomplish something. Your first steps in a new group in which you are a peer are important. Enter the room early and place your papers at a strategic place at the table, preferably at either end of a rectangular table. If some chairs are more impressive than others, choose the most impressive. Once the group gathers, your initiating skill should come into play. Get things started by proposing that the group undertake a task, define a problem, suggest a procedure, and reach conclusions. Some groups will sit for hours with no one taking a strong initiative. This allows a stagnation and bits of minutiae obscure significant matters. The group concludes at the lowest common denominator, which usually means maintaining the status quo.

Another important skill for you to practice is to seek information or opinions from others and to listen honestly to their answers. Most people rarely ask questions of others, yet it's the quickest way to achieve status in the group. And it's the best way to win your own position when you later make your case. If you really listen thoughtfully and without prejudgment, you invariably learn something. You may also learn only that the person is a dolt but this can save valuable time.

Learn to summarize at the proper time. Put in the ideas of others, restating something that has been said perhaps in a simpler way. Offer a conclusion that the group may be moving toward and that is increasingly laced with your action—rooted position. A good technique is to write down a resolution while the others are talking. In achieving consensus, your personal influence will be increased, and they will respect you for it.

Without being pushy, you can help set standards—to suggest guidelines that the group should adhere to in getting its work done. Such things as having an agenda, sticking to it, starting and finishing on time, summarizing what it has accomplished during the time period, defining the problem, and so on, can give you status (power) and ensure results in the group.

With the skills of opinion seeking, initiating, summarizing, and standard setting, the group will be productive. Members will have a heightened self-esteem from the achievement and they will appreciate the individual who set the standard.

The Size of the Group

The size of the group is important. For example, if you really want to work at problem solving, a group as large as 30 is unwieldy and makes the goal impossible. There can be no fruitful interactions at this level. But what a group of 30 can do is listen to a presentation and critique. They might also give suggestions, but no group leader can guide such a sizeable group to any important consensus. It won't fly, so don't try it. If a working group has any chance at all, it should include between five and seven people. This is a large enough body to have divergent points of views, but small enough to allow for healthy participation and a final, firm conclusion.

Handling Conflict

When there is conflict in the group, and particularly against your position, you must convey honest respect for your opponents. You can do this by listening carefully to the opposing position, repeating it in your own words, agreeing with points that you find acceptable, and finally integrating his position into yours. Do this thoughtfully and you'll have your opponent hooked. Remember, charm him or her and let the individual volunteer support for you with no coercion. If you use these skills, you will move faster in getting to "yes." Equally important, you will have developed a way of handling conflict that puts you on top. You will, by example, teach others to do the same. Even if they don't wish to learn, you're ahead of the game because you used persuasion rather than force, which creates resentment and enemies. You will be known as someone who can lead when differences need to be confronted and resolved—you're a negotiator rather than a dictator.

Using Special Groups

There will be times when you'll want to use special groups to come up with creative solutions. It is here that working groups work best. For example, there are times when you simply want to get as many good ideas as you can on the table. This requires drawing together key people known for their analytic abilities and responsiveness. This approach can be effective if done properly.

Initially, brainstorming is a colloquialism for creative problem solving. In the beginning, rule out all evaluative comments. Just let group members fire away as one idea suggests another. Write down their suggestions. Within 15 minutes, a good group can come up with 50 or 60 suggestions, which can then be sorted out to determine how many quality ideas there are. The important point here is that, for a time, you hold your position so that people can be spontaneous. It is difficult for the creative juices to flow in either a highly competitive or judgmental atmosphere. If you are the clearly established leader, encourage unconventional ideas, emphasizing quantity as well as quality. Focus on one problem at a time and don't allow anyone to promote or explain solutions. Just get everyone involved and accustomed to thinking in terms of innovation rather than plodding along in well-worn grooves.

When You Are Clearly the Group Leader

In situations where you are clearly the group leader, carefully structure your meetings. At staff meetings, for example, staff members should participate on your terms, which you announce at your first meeting and gently reinforce at the slightest infraction. Try to meet weekly or at least every ten days. You should have a prearranged substantive agenda, established and approved by you and not by staff. You should sit in the same seat at the most desirable end of a rectangular table. The meeting should always begin with a report from you and should always include uplifting and elevating remarks. Celebrate your product and praise your winners. Then move into the more mundane agenda, but never let the meeting become bogged down in trivia, like housekeeping details. Ask participants to be succinct and alert. Cut off the ramblers because they monopolize and demoralize a group. After sufficient time, end discussion and declare a course of action. Don't obviously strive for consensus judgments, but do your best not to let your decisions offend unnecessarily.

Resist the "we" syndrome. It is only natural for strong sub-managers to try to creep carefully into your authority or power base. The most subtle and effective person might say things like, "Shouldn't we do this...?" or "Didn't we decide at the last meeting...?" Don't let it slide by. The first time it happens, say firmly with a smile, "We don't decide anything," that should be sufficient.

Be careful also of inattentive staff members. These persons seem preoccupied; they may read nonpertinent material; gaze out of the window, and so on. This is especially inconsiderate when you are speaking. Don't say anything at the time, but after the meeting, ask the person to step into your office and tell them that such behavior is both rude and unacceptable.

Start and conclude your meetings on time. Always inject and grant appropriate humor, and your staff meetings will be worthwhile and happy experiences.

If you are already the CEO or a high-ranking division officer, you will find that group meetings with rank and file subordinates can significantly contribute to your charismatic leadership. Here again, design and structure are important. Occasionally, perhaps every six weeks or so, have your assistant or your secretary randomly select 15 to 20 employees from all but top executive ranks of your organization. You need this many present for give and take. Hold the meeting in a warm and impressive area in which you are most comfortable. As each person enters the meeting, greet him or her with a warm personal welcome. Light refreshments should be available. Pay attention to details. A rectangular table is preferable. If chairs are set up, don't have rows. Instead, circle them, with your own chair being somewhat apart and only fairly obvious. After a brief period to allow the participants to get settled comfortably, call the group to order. Make an opening statement in which you express your special mission or dream for the organization and express your good fortune at being associated with such exceptional people. Finally, identify the major issues that confront the organization today. Say all of this with enthusiasm, confidence, and warmth. Then start discussion by asking a question of a supportive member of the group. Let the comments continue for no more than an hour. Avoid extraneous discussions, because you must always remain in positive control. Should any critical comments be made, gently but firmly (before the tenor of the meeting changes) suggest to the speaker that you'd be happy to speak further on this point in person later. These situations are best handled routinely through "open office hours" during which any person may come in without appointment and discuss any subject with you. Conclude the meeting at the predesignated time with a brief inspiring statement of your confidence in your stated goals and the ability of your associates to make positive contributions.

Enough on groups. Consider these suggestions thoughtfully and your groups will always be helpful to you. They just might be productive. Value your time and try not to hold or attend any more meetings than absolutely necessary.

The Art of Silence

When you speak, know what you're talking about. If you want to be influential, you can no longer enjoy the luxury of spontaneous brilliance or foolishness. To be off base on one simple fact, even an unimportant one, is to cast doubt on your credibility. Practice silence and probe the comfortable aspects of this style. Don't be afraid to leave a meeting without having spoken, but try to avoid such meetings in the future. Speaking too often in a business setting is a sign of personal insecurity and in time people won't take you seriously. When you do speak, be succinct, know your facts, and make your statement action-oriented as well analytical. This will cause you to speak dynamically, to listen, and to learn. In time you will be perceived as wise and inspiring.

- Be brilliant; failing that, shut up!
- Seeing may not be believing.
- It is the things we believe but cannot see that are most important to us.
- Never speak to a subordinate as your equal unless you are prepared to be treated as an equal in all things.

- At times, it will serve you well to become abstract in order to appear profound.
- Take the center seat.
- Stand when you speak. If you do it right, only you will know that your feet are in sand.

Other Social Institutions and Power

Without the aid of prejudice and custom, I should not be able to find my way across the room.

—William Hazlitt

A university does great things, but there is one thing it does not do: it does not intellectualize its neighborhood.

—J. H. Newman

Truth rests with God alone, and a little bit with me.

—Yiddish Proverb

It is easy to know God so long as you do not tax yourself with defining Him.

—Joseph Joubert

Patriotism is the last refuge of a scoundrel.

—Dr. Samuel Johnson

You can learn much about power by closely examining our most enduring social institutions. The pulpit, the political platform, and the lectern fairly reek of power. Grand as these great social institutions may be, however, religion, politics, and education have known tragic epochs when their power was corrupted. Debauched leadership has forced millions of human beings to be killed and enslaved and to suffer the most deplorable forms of deprivation. Everything can be perverted by abuse. But all of these institutions are valuable to you.

Religion: The Most Sophisticated Charismatic Social Institution

If you're interested in power, you should study and observe religion. No human social institution has endured so long or been so important in human affairs. Yet it is rooted exclusively in trust and confidence born of faith. Religion magnificently employs and portrays all of the power forms from an assumption that is questionable to many. No social institution in history has so completely established the truth of referent power or charisma as religion. The Christian apostle, Paul, wrote, *"The letter killeth but the spirit maketh live."* So it has been for thousands of years. Religious institutions have endured the abuse of false prophets, the insincerity of political opportunists, and the scorn of intellectuals.

The Roman Seneca wrote, *"Religion for the masses is necessary, for the politician it is useful and for the intellectual is foolish."* Yet many will say there is no evidence corroborating the legitimacy of religion. Absolutely fascinating, isn't it, yet religion has represented the strongest and boldest example ever of the use of power. Primarily through use of charismatic power, religious institutions have checked, inspired, and punished human behavior, created nations, taken and sacrificed lives, and fought wars. Remember this as you address your life.

While all religions are powerful forces, in the United States, the most acceptable—those having the most implied powers are in priority order: Episcopal, Presbyterian, Lutheran, Methodist, and Baptist. Both Catholicism and Judaism run the gambit of implied power and Islam is rapidly gaining strength.

To appreciate the power in religious institutions, you should pay close attention to everything: furniture (particularly the pulpit[s]), flags, religious symbols, windows, ritualized prayers and oaths, baptisms, the dress of the priests and priestesses, the language, the music, and so on. Everything reinforces the belief. Nothing reflects this power more than seeing the entire family, grandparents, parents, and children walking solemnly into their religious institution, dressed in their finery, each carrying a copy of their prayer book. The generations are bound together by their belief in the power of a deity. The temple stands as a monument to what can be done through the intangible forces of power. Indeed, if religious institutions are ever undone, it will not be by other religions; they've been fighting one another since the beginning. In fact, religious institutions will be undone only when the masses no longer need to rely on a power outside themselves. Since there is no suggestion that this is possible, religion will probably remain as long as human beings exist.

But what about religion and you? If you lean toward agnosticism, would a faith enrich your life? I feel very strongly about my own experience, but each person should make this decision only after much thought. It helps for the people you lead and for you to have a religion because it means that they will have a common bond with you. It also makes them accept difficult conditions. And for you, religion can be personally sustaining.

Religious belief can be one of the most sustaining experiences of your life. Religion can help you to explain the things beyond comprehension. You need an infinite resource that you can turn to when all human support fails, as is inevitable.

I'd advise that you stay with the religion of your youth if it is at all consistent with your current thinking. It was integrated into your thinking when you were most dependent and inclined to accept any form of nurturing and authority. Being childlike and suspending scientific scrutiny is about the only way for you to get the fullest inspiration from the religious experience. Think as you will but remember Paul's teaching, "...*the spirit maketh live.*" If you are inclined to investigate a new religion or a new acceptable denomination, remember that the convert is never truly admitted to the club in long-established congregations. If your lifelong religion enhances your life, stay with your roots. You'll stay in contact with the people and yourself by so doing.

Finally, be cautious of your religious institution. Don't confuse it with the full embodiment of your faith. And don't expect your priests (by whatever title) to be completely untainted. They are human. Yes, you should attend your religious institution. If you stay away, you're likely to lose touch with spiritual reflection as well as the social enhancement it can provide. Like any other entity on earth, religion can enlighten or it can be carried to extremes.

In religion, don't let any of human creations stand between you and your faith, but believe.

Play Politics and Float to Power

Your sure-fire way to influence a politician is to get the support of the people who support the politician. Politics is an extraordinary power force. Its roots most obviously are in its charismatic ability to inspire trust and confidence. But unless you decide to actually enter politics, you are wise to play both sides of the street. What you want to do is use the political system to your advantage—to the advantage of your business, your university, your profession, and your cause. Don't blindly assume that only one political party can serve you or that "your" party will always be in

> ### Go to the People Behind the Politician
>
> During my years as a president, I, accompanied by a small entourage, would show up at political fund raisers for both parties. We would work the house and an assistant would try to arrange for me to say a few words. We tried to attend these kinds of meetings for key elected officials all over the state. We met the people behind the politicians and in the process, they also became my people. Never once did any of them refuse a reasonable request of ours.

power. Instead, put your money on every horse that could win so that, regardless of the outcome, you will have a voice in the current political order. Periods of reform or reaction will therefore not affect your power as much.

I've always found George Washington's advice in his farewell address to be sound. He made two main points. This man who could have been king cautioned his fellow Americans against creating *any* political parties and entangling foreign alliances. While good men and women may enter political life, to succeed consistently in politics is to compromise, at first issues, and finally principles. By that time most politicians become walking, talking facades. Remember, few politicians could get a better job out of politics. As I have suggested, it's not that good men and women don't enter politics. Many do. Often initially inspired by the beauty of ancient Grecian political philosophy and a sincere commitment to serve, they come under increasing pressure to compromise. Only the most stable and powerful can remain clean. Just as public service tends to be inefficient, so does the nature of elected political office lead eventually to ethical compromise. Bear in mind, I am not talking solely about compromising on issues. Everyone who is at all intelligent and engaged in life must do that. I'm talking about compromising on values, ideals, morality, *ethics*. Next comes the facade, the hollow you.

Politics contains the inherent weakness of compromise, and the longer you remain in office, the more intense the pressures become to compromise. Now there may be exceptions in political life. I've known a few, and they were the least effective politicians I have known. They were considered mavericks and, therefore, untrustworthy.

Business, education, and religions are more comfortable career choices for you, although a person of power forever faces moral, seductive pressures. You can play and win the power game only by maintaining a flexibility, showing a willingness to listen to all but keeping compromise to a minimum so that you retain your integrity.

Bearing this in mind, heed this advice on how to control politicians, for your work may

Ride Politics to Power

In 1977, I seriously considered running for Governor of my state. A campaign committee was formed and we registered in the Capitol as "Campaign '78." We got underway and the prospect began to look better and better. Money appeared to be the only real question, but as time passed special interest money loomed as essential, yet all of them expected something in return for their support, all of them! Dr. Edgar Berman, an advisor of mine who had also been counsel to Hubert Humphrey, told me, "Do what Hubert did. Take their money, get elected and then do what you will." Nonetheless, by the Christmas season I decided not to run.

After that, members of the State Republican Central Committee asked for a meeting in my office where they urged me to run as a Republican and advised me that they could produce the necessary money with no strings. But by that time, I had decided that elected office was not for me.

require it. I have already suggested that you should play both sides of the street to have some influence with both parties.

Cultivate the politician's major contributors. Attend fund raisers in the politician's district, move around, shake hands, go or send representatives to political clubs, write newspaper articles, do radio and television, even advertise. Remember that the politician's people can also be your people.

If you go only the route of making political contributions and entertaining elected officials, you will remain a pawn of the elected official. You will not be powerful, but rather you will depend on the power of this official. Elected officials and staff members often are rude and insufferably arrogant, even to major contributors, especially those who do not come from their home bases. You will suffer their condescending behavior if you value their support. Sometimes you don't get even their vote. You will keep throwing good money after bad in hope for support.

There will always be those who simper in our nation's capitals, currying favor with pompous, compromised elected officials, people who understand little about the political process they are trying to influence. You must be one of the smart ones. You can beat them hands down and you won't have to compromise anything. And it is gratifying to use the process properly and ethically. You will demonstrate the effects of power sensibly applied and emerge absolutely untainted. And remember, if you would be powerful, pretend to be powerful.

Education: Both Perceived and Real Power

Education plays a role in your power course, although not enough and not in the right way. But it does play a role. Education (expert power) in terms of knowledge is one of the most effective ways to influence, even more effective than punishment, reward, or even legitimized authority. The kind of education that I am talking about here is the kind that contributes to your legitimate power, deserved or not.

The "right" school does make a difference, but you can easily overcome having attended a college with a second-rate image. So while you should know this, don't take it too seriously. You can make it regardless of where you went to college. Do not think for a moment that you get a better education at Harvard than Northwestern Wyoming State. You can get a fine education wherever there is an adequate library and a few active minds. Ours is a superficial society. It automatically grants legitimacy to symbols: a religious collar, gold braid, pin-stripe suits, Mercedes Benz motorcars, presidents, and Harvard. So if you have a choice, go to Harvard or one of its many images: The Ivy League, The Seven

Sisters (single-sex schools are always in vogue), Stanford, Chicago, Duke, Cornell, Northwestern, Notre Dame, and Georgetown. Even public institutions can be Harvards— like Virginia, Michigan, University of North Carolina, Wisconsin, or Berkeley. For the smaller, deadly serious versions of Harvard, try Williams, Davidson, Amherst, Washington and Lee, Carleton, Centre, Claremont, Hamilton, and "oh" Reed.

You can't go wrong at any of the universities included in the elite and ultra conservative American Association of Universities. Some institutions jockey for years just to be considered for membership. You can get a list by writing to their Washington, D.C. office. Remember, it's an appropriately elitist world, but with many false values. Don't admit it publicly, but don't kid yourself either, because good or bad, coming from the right school can make a difference.

If you realize this too late or if other circumstances prevent selecting these kinds of institutions, it's not too late. Pick one of these institutions for an advanced degree, an MBA, LL.D., a Ph.D. or even a short summer course. Today, in spite of a market glut, an MBA is the best master's degree. If you read this ten years from now, check around for what's in vogue. A Mickey Mouse degree from a "good" college or university is still a joke. When you get your advanced degree from such an institution, you will never be quite as acceptable but at least "they" will know that you know better. Most importantly, you will know that after mastering the best they have to offer, they're not so smart after all.

Many, because of social and economic reasons, attend small private colleges or regional public universities and then take advanced degrees from more prestigious schools. And they often conclude that the intellectual rigor of their undergraduate school was infinitely more demanding than that of the name school. The name school teaches confidence without bravado and too often other schools teach about how to humbly and gladly accept whatever. The ambience of the name school can make a quiet but telling statement about power and authority, about being somebody. The attitude conveyed of too many institutions says quietly but too effectively, "accept your lot...don't rock the boat." You can overcome this, but you need to know it first.

You must remember that you are only as average as you think you are, and don't let anyone tell you that being average is your lot. For the most part, it is best to stay out of environments that send such messages. You have a potential to be unique and the judgment of others can often be wholly misleading.

Next in the educational power-pecking order are the good, but not big name, liberal arts colleges and the "other" land-grant universities: Grinnell, Millikin, Carroll, Loyola, Dickinson, Hollins, Hood and hundred or so others. Most small liberal arts colleges are good. The average land-grants include Indiana, Ohio State, Nebraska, Michigan State, Penn State, Florida, Maryland, Alabama, Oklahoma, and 20 or so other pennant-waving, football-playing Neanderthals. You will have to press to become educated at one of these institutions, but you can do it. However, they do carry a certain provincial prestige and a power message. But with good organization and intellectual curiosity, you can get a splendid education at almost any college or university in the country. Those who blame the college for their educational difficulties are missing the real culprit.

Next on the power pole are the regional public colleges and universities. These places are usually quite serious about teaching and faculty members engage in sufficient research activities to stay in touch with their teaching fields. Some even teach 12 to 15 hours a week. Unfortunately, most of these institutions are trying foolishly to emulate the land-grants and as they become more successful they become less effective.

By and large, these regional publics are the places that have converted more plowboys (and girls) and blue-collar city kids and downright poor people into intellectuals than any kind of institution in history. They are probably the best proof of the Western world's social mobility. Again, it's unfortunate that more of their graduates don't realize how good the institutions really are and how little they as graduates differ intellectually from students from the "best" institutions. They're generally smaller and more obviously committed to teaching than their land grant mentors.

Incidentally, ordinarily you may assume that the smaller a college is, the better it is for you. This is particularly true if the institution has sufficient resources plus the good sense to have relatively small classes. Would you rather talk to Socrates one-on-one or one-on-500? I once taught a psychology class of 500; the experience was a contradiction in terms. Small colleges also tend to be confidence builders. They give you more leadership and power opportunities, especially those in the Midwest.

Lastly, there are the public community colleges, the institutions where some excellent teaching goes on. About all the faculty members are expected to do is teach. If they occasionally wander, the average student is mature enough to nudge the teacher back to the job. Unfortunately, most of those institutions are getting too large. And this, coupled with their localism, make any real sense of community all but impossible. There are few leadership opportunities and

Community College Breeds Academic Success

At Piedmont Community College in Virginia students often transfer to the prestigious selective University of Virginia. On the average they do better than students who enroll at the University as freshmen. Most of the Piedmont students could not have been admitted to the University of Virginia as freshmen.

almost no out-of-class confidence builders. These institutions care, but you should know that you're pretty much on your own there and that the subculture won't give you much support. There are exceptions, of course. Rogers State College in Claremont, Oklahoma, for example, blows my generalizations out of the water. There, you find a public community college with all the flavor of a good, small liberal arts college. But don't expect to find anything like that in most other states.

Remember this about public two-year colleges: their graduates go on to "major" universities and frequently do as well or better than the students who enrolled in the major universities as freshmen. If you look for confidence building elsewhere, you can get a first-rate education at many community colleges.

Then there are the private two-year colleges. Although they associate together professionally, they are almost completely unlike public two-year schools. The one thing both have in common is generally excellent teaching, but the private two-year college is closer in nature to a good, small liberal arts college.

Regardless of the type of school, effective corporate leaders tend to have majored in the social sciences and humanities rather than mathematics, engineering, or any of the "pure" sciences. Of course, there are some startling exceptions. This doesn't mean that if you didn't major in English, it's too late. But you might take a few postgraduate courses or at least start a systematic program of self-study and broad social exposure.

Finally, always remember the fundamental value of education. It is the root and flower of your expert power, and along with your charisma, the key to your ultimate achievements. Just remember that you can be educated anywhere, in or out of school. Know that education must go on for your entire lifetime. And remember that you will have a slight edge in legitimate power if you go to the "right" school.

- Don't be too impressed with Harvard or other impressive credentials. Learn to judge by performance that you yourself observe.
- The great, terrible, important powers of the world, like social caste and domination of religions, always rest on secrets. Don't try to find them out; pretend you know them.

Characteristics of the Effective Organization

Where there is no vision, the people perish.

—Proverbs

Living movements do not come of committees.
—J. H. Newman

He that leaveth nothing to chance will do few things ill, but he will do very few things.

—Lord Halifax

What follows will be your primer to expert power within the organization. Read carefully. Commit the thirteen characteristics that follow to memory, for they will serve you well in almost any corporate setting, company, military, government, education, religion etc.

They will also serve as effective reminders should you, from time to time, get carried away with either popular or esoteric techniques like TQM or re-engineering. (They are not really too esoteric for you to understand. They are usually fair ideas considered because others of importance—especially those in power—seem to accept them, so you feel that you should also.) Be respectfully skeptical of any new corporate concept until it makes complete sense to you. In time, people will think you are brilliant. Remember in any organization, leadership is far more important than process. Too many executives believe that a new technique or method will save them; without leadership, whatever the process, it will finally fail.

There are countless books and articles on organizational characteristics. Most people mistakenly assume that these "typical" characteristics are also the features of effective corporations. This is the reason that most corporations, profit and non-profit, are mediocre in performance. It may also explain why some other nations have surpassed Americans in both efficiency and quality. During recent years, there have been more enlightened efforts to assess the distinguishing characteristics of especially effective corporations. These studies didn't simply identify conditions and individuals that characterize corporations in general; they look at the best, not everybody. The difference between the two is dramatic. Always remember this simple truth: *there is a marked difference between the average of a general condition and the average of an excellent condition.* You want to be the best of the best.

> **From J.P. Morgan to Ray Kroc**
>
> "The characteristics of effective organizations haven't changed much over the years. The past century has easily been the most frenetically paced in history. Leadership, mission, service, ingenuity, organization, competition and salesmanship were qualities that ranged from J.P. Morgan's calming the panic of 1907 to Ray Kroc's 'billions and billions' served." (*Fortune*, November 1999)

Use this list because it will help you for your lifetime. Use it as a point of departure in your work and people will consider you consistently astute. Now the lucky thirteen:

1. Leadership

The most constant characteristic of the effective corporation is strong transforming leadership. This leadership is rooted in a thoughtful understanding and appreciation of the nature and use of power and its sensitive application—in effect what this book is about. Unfortunately, of more than a dozen recent popular (best selling) paradigms I examined, few seriously considered leadership. Only two considered power, something leaders can't do without. Remember that leadership without power is a contradiction in terms.

If leadership is important at all levels of an organization, it is an imperative at the top. In terms of impact it can be quiet or flamboyant, but above all things, it should be *obvious*. It doesn't really matter whether the leader is slanted right or left or down the middle. The leader stands confidently for the corporate mission within a greater context of God, country, prosperity, and apple pie. Assuming these things then, confident leaders can get away with just about anything. They can challenge ineffective but established orthodoxies and practices. They can dramatically reorganize the department or the division and in time the corporation. Overnight, they can change ancient procedures and practices. They can do almost anything within reason.

Leaders like this are apt to be called bold, assertive, and perhaps aggressive. Although their productiveness and charm keep getting them promotions until they are firmly established on top, their corporate peers sometimes consider them loose cannons. You can never quite tell what this leader will say or do. But you can bet he or she will be where the action is—probably at the center of it.

Being this kind of leader requires only that you be reasonably well educated (be able to read, write, and speak coherently), of average or average-plus

Be a Lion

"It's better to have one lion in charge of 10,000 rabbits than one rabbit in charge of 10,000 lions."
—Napoleon

intelligence, and intensely motivated. You were *not* born with this extraordinary quality. *You* can develop it.

2. Action

The effective leader in the effective corporation must be willing to act. So for Pete's sake, do something! Don't cower in uncertainty, afraid to act because you may make a mistake or invade someone's domain. People are rarely fired for doing. Beware of meetings, long range plans, and anything about expensive technology (computers) that you don't readily understand but remember technology is tomorrow. Know it and use it. Get an MBA, but don't make a dogma of your courses. Pay attention, but be skeptical of anything that smacks of matrix management, technical rationality, or invasive strategic planning. You need to be knowledge-able, but copy no popular approach. You may miss a few targets, but you'll hit the greater num-ber. Learn from your misses. Don't dote on them and keep moving.

Run from Day One

Hit the ground running, or else is the advice of *Right from the Start* (Harvard Business Review Press 2000) noting that two/thirds of the outsiders appointed presidents since 1993 have left their positions with-in four years because they didn't take charge and move from the get-go.

You must always be doing something designed to be more pro-ductive or make things better. Regardless of position, view dubi-ously everyone not involved in positive action. Often they are obstacles to progress. Spend as little time talking as possible.

3. Educated Intuition

And how does the effective corporate leader act? Out of edu-cated intuition! As leader, make your decisions based on your deep commitment, your thoughtful judgment, and your past experi-ence. Don't spend much time on issue-begging, long-range, or strategic plans, most of them are as useless as they are costly. Read, listen, study your competition, make decisions. Beyond projected production figures based on maximum market potential, there is no need for you to be concerned with anything other than making your area of responsibility the finest of its kind. The great measure of your planning should be over a brief time period, a year or less. Your objectives should be both general and specific. The specific objectives allow for measurements. The general ones allow for spontaneous action and growth on your part and that of your team. Remember, educated intuition means that you have saturat-ed yourself with information about your business and you are ready and willing to act. You don't need further detailed confir-mation or analysis. Stop worrying. Plan, but don't spend much time or money on it. Take a risk. Decide. Act!

A final word here. If you have a boss smitten by the momen-tary currency of complicated, time-consuming strategic planning, be a bit more equivocal about your position, but don't sell out completely. In time it won't work for the boss and you don't want to be blamed for his or her slow enlightenment.

4. A Passionate Mission

The effective organization has a mission about which you are passionate. Passion is something innate in you. It must be something far greater—God, country, basic goodness, and the welfare of the individual. One mission-driven, excellent U.S. corporation offered products at a loss in Japan just because the CEO thought the U.S. should be there. You not only want to be the most profitable of your kind but, even more, you want to be the very best of your kind. And if you are the very best, you will be the most profitable in the long run. Whatever it is that you do, you must believe that it improves the human condition. If you don't believe it, do something else.

As a leader, you will communicate your passion and your willingness to act on your dream to all who come into contact with you in groups and casual conversa-

> **The Case for Passion**
>
> Nike CEO, Phil Knight, transformed Nike into a marketing machine. He emphasized emotion and re-invention—continuous re-invention. Richard Terrlink of Harley Davidson sold American nostalgia. Amgen, Home Depot, Intel, and Champion all appealed to feeling. Starbucks took a sleeping supermarket commodity—coffee—and began selling it in infinite varieties in trendy stores, thereby establishing a whole new market.

tion. You are alive with your calling. People may even call you evangelical. They called Jack Welch "fanatical" and Warren Buffett "magical." Good, you're on your way.

5. Service

Already implied and now more boldly emphasized—that's service. Service to consumers, clients, students, members, troops, voters, etc, must be more important to you than immediate bottom-line. You define nearly every corporate activity in terms of service to the consumer. This means that you maintain and make good on your product after the sale, even if it momentarily costs you money. Do this, have a reasonably good accounting system, and bottom-line profits will be more impressive than your projections.

You must think of people as individuals, *one at a time*, and the extent to which your product serves their interests and needs. Ask yourself *"How will it play with my favorite uncle in Peoria?"* Remember, first and finally, you define your decisions in terms of service to your consumer, be he or she customer, citizen, client, patient, or student.

6. Structure

The really excellent corporation has a formal organization within which you behave in a consistently courteous and warm manner. There will be a chairman to whom the president reports, vice presidents who report to the president, managers or directors who report to the vice presidents, and so on. Rarely cross this line of delegated authority, and then only gently to remind subordinates implicitly that you still have that power. It's a remarkable form of quality control. Vice presidents don't go to the chairman. Managers don't go to the president, but the chairman and the president can go wherever they want. Your function within this formal organization is to accept and support it or quit, and within its structure, behave effectively and in good spirit.

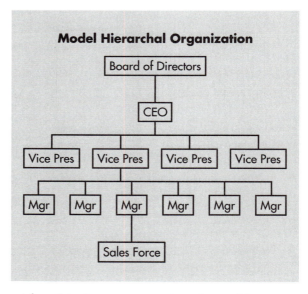

Model Hierarchal Organization

Board of Directors

CEO

Vice Pres · Vice Pres · Vice Pres · Vice Pres

Mgr · Mgr · Mgr · Mgr · Mgr · Mgr

Sales Force

For instance, it is perfectly acceptable for you as the president or the manager or department head to be warm and caring with members of the staff. But you must always convey the fact, without being officious, of your position. And you must not undercut or override the prerogatives of those who report to you. To constantly ignore lines of authority is to invite those around you to follow your lead.

Behave spontaneously and warmly while always reinforcing the organization's formal and clear management or administrative structure. Ultimately staff will consider you loyal, enlightened, and productive. Leave it to others to dabble in the politics of the corporation.

Remember the opening analogy of St. Simone. Imagine yourself on your platform. Take a chair, stand on it, but only then sit in a relaxed, self-effacing style. You will be assailed by many office experiences, but stay on your chair. Imagine yourself being on that chair wherever you are in your formal organization. Now you've got it. Just don't get off!

The current literature notes at least two other types of corporate organizations—the collegial and the personalistic. The collegial has little formal authority vested in its officers. It tries to make expertise the prime determinant of corporate influence and teamwork the condition that holds down conflict. Collegial organizations tend to be some high-tech firms, partnership organizations, many colleges and universities, hospitals, and other places where there are many professional employees. In the profit-making world, in time, these organizations will change or fail, and in the not-for-profit, they should be audited and governed more carefully.

Even though high-tech firms continue to enjoy popular favor (although a number are beginning to have problems), we cannot ignore their basic inefficiencies. The collegial model can only work in an organization when its goal or assignments are clear and specific and when the numbers of staff are relatively small and each individual is accountable; the more people involved, regardless of their professional level, the more the organization needs a formal structure. Remember Chapter 2 on Legitimate Power.

The personalistic corporate models are the new entrepreneurial, fast-growing corporations. Here, the individual is all but completely autonomous—with no regard for corporate structure or others in the company. There is no limit on staff expertise. And so long as the boom lasts, there is happiness. In time, the company dies or adopts a more formal corporate model. If it isn't too big, it may become collegial and still survive. But size demands form and structure. Indeed, history proves that the formalistic model, within which one may behave rather informally, is better regardless of the nature or size of the organization.

7. An Organizational Culture

Another specific feature of the excellent corporation is a strong personal identification with the organization by employees. People are pleased, even proud to be associated. While members of this kind of corporation may at times be argumentative

A Corporate Culture

Fifty years ago I enlisted in the Marine Corps for three years. I am still a Marine.

among themselves, they take exception when outsiders find fault.

And yours should be an almost poetic commitment, one that goes beyond facts and figures, salary and prerequisites, and momentary adversity. (Remember I said poetic—not zealous or blind.) Until it actually happens, just behave as though the organization were yours. And remember you have to put *a lot in* before you start getting anything out. In spite of what others may do, don't pad your expense account, cheat on time expectations, or moan about how little you get for how much you do.

As you move up the organizational ladder, there are a number of things you can do to foster your organizational culture.

First and foremost, know that in the eyes of all below you, you are the corporation. You can do this without being perceived as disloyal to your supervisors. Just weave your support for them into your style. When you get to the top, the smart ones will do the same for you.

Compare yourself with your competition. Define every possible comparison and outperform them in every measure. Get everybody in your company in on the act and share the results.

The formal corporate structure and your personal social distance will serve you well here. Don't violate either. Do so and you may be immediately popular and even momentarily productive. But in time, the whole structure you have compromised will come falling down on the overexposed you. Within this formal/informal structure, employees must know that you are the personification of the company and really care about their best interests. You inspire them as you direct them to greater service and production. You use letters of praise, corporate ceremonies, bonuses, and personal thank-you's. You do these things at every opportunity.

There are other factors that mark an organizational culture—flags; success celebrations; impressive, immaculate buildings, offices and other work stations. It's wise to allow chances for employees to invest in but not control the corporation. And don't underestimate apparently unimportant things like appropriate professional decorum and dress.

No matter what you've heard, these things rarely contribute to a healthy

> **From the Memoirs of a Successful Sea Captain**
>
> If you are going on a long voyage, be sure that your crew members know their boundaries. From the first day on board make courtesy and respect for one another bywords. Give them grog only on special occasions and then only just before they sleep. At the end of a successful voyage, they will be happy together and they will love you and their ship.

corporate culture: most office parties, company athletic teams, large employee/officer cafeterias or lounges, and any outside social meetings between company members. Stick to your business. You'll get to know each other well enough.

8. The Common Touch

Leaders of effective organizations remain in touch with the people they lead. Some have called this management by moving around or roving. The key is *how* you move around. The leader isn't chained to the executive desk. Get out with the people. In the plant, it's with the workers as well as the executives. In the store, with the sales personnel. In the university, it means talking to the maintenance crew and students as well as faculty. In the military, you relate to the soldier or sailor as the leader. You do this by moving up and down the ranks within the organization. Get out of the office.

Occasionally have lunch in the employees' cafeteria or have a beer in the tavern across the street. You can be congenial and yet never "one of the guys." But only occasionally. They don't want you around all the time. They do the work. As leader, your job is to inspire them—to be one of them, but apart from them. They expect their leader to be more than they are and if they know you too well, they won't follow. This is where you are a friendly phantom. You are everywhere and nowhere. Be with them to know and let them know that you care about them as well as your product.

Show up on the assembly line and in out-of-the-way offices. Visit hospitals and attend funerals. Stop by and see an employee who has just achieved an impressive record. Try to make a point of showing up where you are least expected at

> **Thick and Thin**
>
> After I was out of office a few years, those who remembered me best and most fondly were the custodians, the secretaries, and the maintenance workers. I felt the same way about them. They supported me through thick and thin.

least once a week. Keep your appearances brief, warm, and inspiring. Your charismatic power within your organization will affect morale and production in ways that will stagger even your own expectations.

9. Importance of the Individual Employee

In the long run, every effective corporation has a leader who places as much importance on the worth and dignity of the individual employee as on the corporation itself. Beware of the person who says, "I did it in the best interest of the company." This person may stab you next. The only time the company supersedes the employee is when the survival of the company is at stake unless employees are cut back. Then the decision must be made in view of the greater number of surviving employees. But, in the final analysis, the burden of quality or representation depends on the individual worker. This means that to motivate them, you as leader must offer competitive salaries, bonuses, employee investment in the corporation, impressive health and medical benefits, retirement plans (also early retirement programs), holidays, and vacations.

Every person in the organization should do a job that is important to the company and deserves respect and thoughtful attention. The company appreciates the fundamental role of the individual and makes it possible for that person to produce in pride and appreciation. That person is precious.

As the leader, you must think of every person as worthy and deserving of your serious attention and concern. How also could you regularly ask them to do more for less? If you do these things sincerely you won't have to tell them. They will know it. And they will produce for themselves and for you, the boss who acknowledges their input and values them personally.

This does *not* mean that you harbor or tolerate malcontents, laggards, or incompetents. To do so would be disservice to them more than anyone else. You establish mutually acceptable standards for your people, just as you set for yourself, but they should be realistic. Those who meet and exceed your common goals are the models of the corporation. For those who do not catch the spirit, you must first try to salvage them. Failing that, confront the problem early and directly, and have the person dismissed as gracefully as possible or reassigned out of your sphere of responsibility. But don't ever ignore them because they won't go away on their own accord. And they will infect your entire organization. Bear in mind that defining the corporation in terms of the best interests of the individual producers is not merely a good intention—it's good business. It also pays off in bottom line dollars and cents. A strong structure, strong leadership, and a caring attitude toward your staff reflect the highest form of charismatic expression.

10. Decision Making at the Lowest Possible Level

Within the effective corporation's formal corporate structure, every person should be as autonomous as possible. Every position is important, or it should not exist. And to every extent possible within that formal corporate structure, you as leader must grant the individual interpretation and expression and most of them will strive to offer a unique contribution. Give them a responsibility within the corporate boundaries and judge them by their results rather than your methods. Monitor them, evaluate them, but let them decide. All employees should be given the opportunity and encouragement to be the very best at what they do.

This in no way suggests that you compromise the essential formality of the organization. I recall my years in the U.S. Marine Corps, as formal as any corporate structure. The Marine Corps operates on the premise that every Marine, regardless of rank, is a self-sufficient decision- maker within the sphere of an assignment.

In this spirit, every executive in a corporation should ask this question: Should I make this decision or should someone at the next level down make it? Such a practice not only grants a license to produce and excel throughout the organization, but it also retards that characteristic of the drowning corporation, high-level preoccupation with detail. Be aware of the details, but let someone else do them.

11. Kooks

Effective corporations nurture kooks. One study calls these types "executive champions." Others call them "pathfinders" or "zeros." But those terms are too easy, too comfortable for you, the rising power figure. I call them kooks in the hope of jarring your thinking. I want to get your disciplined and ambitious mind to accept others who are completely unlike you. The happy kook is an imperative in the really excellent corporation. Kooks are the ones who drive us up a wall from time to time with their idiosyncratic approach. They act without regard for form or structure. They repeat mistakes in reasonable management behavior, and they are often as irascible as they are independent.

They are the ones we can never quite classify—neither their personalities nor their ideas. It just happens that given free rein, they may amaze you with their ideas and results. Time after time, they come up with completely new product lines or create advertising campaigns. They create and they extrapolate in their inimitable style. The rest of us copy and interpolate. Most executives by nature and experience like things to be in place, to run smoothly and sensibly, to have everything in order. But not the kook; this is the person who questions almost everything, respecting no sacred cow. If he or she doesn't question, then behavior will not challenge accepted standards.

Charlie

Charlie was a creative grouch. For 15 years he did only his job and snarled when others came too near. People advised his new CEO that it would be best to put a transom on his office door and occasionally throw meat over the transom. However, the new CEO unleashed Charlie throughout the organization; everybody prospered and Charlie was happy for the first time since he joined the company. And, everybody learned to love him.

Given a license by you, this pure dreamer and innovator can provide the margin of excellence for your company. The unleashed kook even has a certain charisma born of genius (expertise) and from this base, can attract a legion of admirers. These will include employees who will extend themselves for the kook. While they are unaware of the value of other power forms, kooks eschew them.

While most of us will give lip service to supporting kooks, few really do. When the kook tests us with bizarre behavior or some outlandish idea, we are apt to say no or equivocate. Naturally, you as leader must discriminate between the virtuoso and the weirdo. An insensitive leader can allow kooks to wander from job to job or let them sit frustrated in a small office, ignored and neglected. Don't let this happen to you.

12. Research

The effective organization invests in research, pure and applied, and frequent literature review (knowing the best current thinking in the field). While the kook points in this direction, research and literature review take both detached perspective and systematic methodology. Pure research is the kind of investigation that seems to have no direct bearing on immediate bottom line profits. It's what some call "scientific blue-skying." In effect, it's research for the sake of research. Over the years, however, it pays off—if not in profits, in promoting a progressive attitude. Applied research relates more directly to production and sales. It includes such things as market analysis, consumer attitude, and quality control.

But research costs money, whatever type is selected. If you organization isn't large or profitable enough to engage in pure research, do applied research. Most of your new ideas will come from carefully and frequently reviewing the best practices in your field—literature review. Someone, including you, must regularly read the best journals in your particular area and attend professional meetings where speakers reveal valuable professional ideas. You might have quarterly reports prepared and critiqued by your top staff in a freewheeling meeting.

Research and professional awareness, like kooks, are components of your "smart" insurance. They are your investment in a good future, for they make it unlikely you will ever get satisfied with your success.

13. Merit Must or Out

The effective corporation seeks out the best employees and rewards them. Americans have forgotten the axioms that put others ahead. Merit must or out. Hire the best people, keep them educated, and pay them more than your competition. In reality, *no* two people are worth exactly the same pay. In your operation, to the extent possible, there should be a wide salary range for each job. And you should base the pay primarily on merit.

To the greatest possible extent, you should determine merit by objective criteria coupled with subjective judgments. In the last analyses, however subjective, you must judge on merit. Make it or your unit or company will produce less.

A tough but good way to determine merit is for the leader to rank order every position under his or her authority in five dimensions: by order of the importance of the job assigned, by order of the job performed, by order of the willingness of the employee to accept or initiate extra assignments, by order of your estimate of how loyal the employee is to you, and by order of how difficult it would be to replace the staff member. You then

Organizational Merit Assessment	
Performance Dimensions (1-10 scale)	Miller
Contribution Performance in the job	
Initiative Willingness to initiate or accept additional assignments	
Loyalty Employee support and commitment to you and your goals	
Replacement Difficulty of replacing this particular employee	
Merit Ratings	
Average Rating	
Compensation Adjustments	
Percent Salary Increase	
Bonus	

have five lists and a lot of light from the comparison. You could then do an overall comparison.

Remember this from Thomas Jefferson when you are besieged by unyielding unionism, unrealistic affirmative action advocates, malcontents, or well-meaning, but naive do-gooders. "The most precious freedom we have is the freedom to become unequal." The opportunity to have a chance to stand out, to be better, to prove that we are exceptional—this is the stuff of dynamism. It produces excellence, the opportunities for personal charisma, and the freedom to develop and express unique individuality.

The excellent corporation not only pays its winners more, but it celebrates them at every possible opportunity. There are formal plaques, trophies, certificates, and notes of appreciation from you. Or you just stop by the winner's work space, saying, "great job!" The intangible but indispensable trait of showing a sincere regard for all co-workers is the mortar that keeps the organization together.

Now bear in mind these Lucky Thirteen points:
1) Leadership
2) Action
3) Educated Intuition
4) A Passionate Mission
5) Service
6) Structure
7) Organizational Culture
8) The Common Touch
9) The Importance of the Individual Employee
10) Decision Making at the Lowest Possible Level
11) Kooks
12) Research
13) Merit
Make decisions based on them and you will move up.

- To be clever is to maintain that our successes are due to Providence and not to our own cleverness.
- Your specific goals should be annual but even they should include the unmeasurable and the visionary.
- The company that isn't going forward is going backward.
- Educated random activity is infinitely more productive than detailed planning. Use, but beware of the strategic planner.

Epilogue

There you have it, a book that lights your way to extraordinary success and reasonable happiness. You are a unique person with the energy, intelligence, and drive to make an exceptional contribution. Follow these canons and you will grow, in both your professional and personal life. When you occasionally misstep, pause, think, and regroup; don't reconcile yourself to something less. Yes, you can have it all or at least a lot more than you thought you could.

Above all things, remember *social distance* which you may tend to question in times of unusual stress or anxiety. Don't do it. To do so will bring you nothing but more frustration, stalemate, and finally, unattractive cynicism.

Always bear in mind the power topology and use it, from least to most effective: *coercion, reward, legitimate, expert* and *charismatic*.

Remember also, leadership is power and power without ethics is venal and self-corrupting and finally leaves one withered and empty without grace or substance.

With these things firmly in mind and at least a 90 percent score on the test in the appendix, you can give this book to a friend who works for another organization.

Appendix

True False

1. The effective use of power is leadership.
2. To be a successful executive, one should be included in the "in" group in the corporation.
3. It is good to socialize with fellow executives.
4. Rising executives should invite the boss to dinner.
5. The effective leader strives to know the personal lives of his employees.
6. Office parties, birthday celebrations, and the like are morale builders.
7. The effective executive delegates everything but final authority.
8. Give competitors something to gossip about.
9. Be wary of going to retirements, funerals, or other "important employee events."
10. Generally, men are more effective leaders than women.
11. Establish close personal relationships with corporate peers.
12. If careful, office romances can be kept secret.
13. A platform (legitimacy) is important to a leader.
14. Be aloof in your work.
15. Women's colleges are best for women who would be leaders.
16. The effective CEO has a board of directors involved in the organization.
17. Mystique plays no role in leadership.
18. Do not listen to corporate dissidents.
19. Social drinking can facilitate your rise up the corporate ladder.
20. Religious institutions convey an extraordinary sense of power.
21. Content and facts play a relatively minor role in effective communication.

_____ _____ 22. If your good work goes unrecognized, tell your boss.

_____ _____ 23. Women executives are generally too easy on other women.

_____ _____ 24. The fast-rising executive will alienate some within the corporation.

_____ _____ 25. High intelligence is a characteristic of senior executives.

_____ _____ 26. The effective leader is primarily concerned about being liked.

_____ _____ 27. The transactional leader is oriented toward significant change.

_____ _____ 28. It is best to be promoted from outside the organization.

_____ _____ 29. When speaking, maximum use of audio-visual aids enhances personal charisma.

_____ _____ 30. The leader always encourages questions during a presentation.

_____ _____ 31. After-dinner speeches are always the most impressive.

_____ _____ 32. If you want to sell something, go as a team.

_____ _____ 33. Most business meetings are productive.

_____ _____ 34. The right school can make an important difference.

_____ _____ 35. You should always speak up in meetings.

_____ _____ 36. Sports lovers are happier and more successful than non-fans.

_____ _____ 37. The best size for a working group is from 13 to 15.

_____ _____ 38. In office meetings, the leader should encourage full and equal participation.

_____ _____ 39. Effective communication is more style than substance.

_____ _____ 40. Mentoring in the corporate world is passé.

_____ _____ 41. Charm and dress are important factors in effective communication.

_____ _____ 42. A board should regularly ask the employees about the effectiveness of their leader.

_____ _____ 43. The "flat" organizational structure is most conducive to employee production.

_____ _____ 44. It doesn't matter what kind of car the rising executive drives.

_____ _____ 45. Office furnishings should be light and airy.

_____ _____ 46. The effective leader freely admits self-doubt.

_____ _____ 47. Joining clubs, civic organizations, and other groups enhances position.

_____ _____ 48. Your resume should be impersonal and professional.

_____ _____ 49. Your spouse should be involved in your work.

_____ _____ 50. The effective leader can usually stay indefinitely.

_____ _____ 51. The effective leader is more concerned about the welfare of the individual than the corporation.

_____ _____ 52. The effective leader is never viewed as flamboyant.

_____ _____ 53. Coercion is an effective form of influence.

_____ _____ 54. Women executives often try to appear more confident in order to gain favor with male executives.

_____ _____ 55. The effective leader becomes deeply involved in community affairs.

_____ _____ 56. Leaders should try to appear more self-effacing and less confident than they are inclined to be.

_____ _____ 57. Socio-economic background continues to play a significant role in creating leaders.

_____ _____ 58. Consensus is the best form of decision-making.

_____ _____ 59. In leadership, gender differences are more striking than individual differences.

_____ _____ 60. The effective leader is often viewed as mysterious.

_____ _____ 61. The leader should try to appear as normal as possible.

_____ _____ 62. The typical CEO in the United States is male or female, usually educated at a private college with an advanced degree from a public university, and is a registered Democrat.

_____ _____ 63. The effective leader uses time efficiently.

_____ _____ 64. The effective leader must stay involved in the details of the organization.

_____ _____ 65. Sophisticated people are as susceptible to leaders as others.

_____ _____ 66. The wise leader never admits a mistake.

_____ _____ 67. The effective leader speaks spontaneously.

_____ _____ 68. The effective leader delegates punishment.

_____ _____ 69. The goals of the leader should always be specific, understandable, and measurable.

_____ _____ 70. Above all things, the effective leader wants to be professionally admired.

_____ _____ 71. Small dinner parties are more effective than larger social functions in enhancing the leader.

_____ _____ 72. The effective leader strongly desires to be accepted.

_____ _____ 73. There is little value in trying to convert an adversary.

_____ _____ 74. The less structure, the easier it is to lead.

_____ _____ 75. The effective leader arrives at a dinner party early and leaves late.

_____ _____ 76. The power to appoint, pay, promote, and punish is the most significant essential of leadership.

_____ _____ 77. Management skills are more important to the leader than a sense of mission.

_____ _____ 78. The leader should strongly identify with the people.

_____ _____ 79. Expertise in the field is more important to the leader than the ability to reward.

_____ _____ 80. Talented people typically have less self-esteem than less talented people.

_____ _____ 81. Good results are more related to organizational structure than the communication of facts.

_____ _____ 82. Position is an important dimension of leadership.

_____ _____ 83. People are more secure with a strong leader.

_____ _____ 84. The effective leader knows and is inclined to the details of the organization.

_____ _____ 85. Appointed leaders are generally less effective than elected leaders.

_____ _____ 86. You should be perceived as an expert in the field.

_____ _____ 87. Legitimate power enhances charisma.

_____ _____ 88. Participative leaders are most influential.

_____ _____ 89. High status is helpful to the leader.

_____ _____ 90. Try to follow a person who did a good job.

_____ _____ 91. People expect you to try to influence them.

(Answers on next page.)

Answers

1. True
2. False
3. False
4. True
5. False
6. False
7. True
8. True
9. False
10. False
11. False
12. False
13. True
14. True
15. True
16. False
17. False
18. False
19. False
20. True
21. True
22. False
23. False
24. True
25. False
26. False
27. False
28. True
29. False
30. False
31. False
32. False
33. False

34. True
35. False
36. True
37. False
38. False
39. True
40. False
41. True
42. False
43. False
44. False
45. False
46. False
47. False
48. False
49. False
50. False
51. True
52. False
53. True
54. False
55. False
56. False
57. False
58. False
59. False
60. True
61. False
62. False
63. True
64. False
65. False
66. False

67. False
68. True
69. False
70. False
71. False
72. False
73. False
74. False
75. False
76. False
77. False
78. True
79. True
80. True
81. True
82. True
83. True
84. False
85. False
86. True
87. True
88. False
89. True
90. False
91. True

Notes

Chapter 1

[1] French, J.R.P., and Raven, B. "The Bases of Social Power." In *Group Dynamics* (3rd ed.), edited by D. Cartwright and A. Zander. New York: Harper & Row, 1968. Although all of the generalizations in this chapter are born of scholarly research, this is not an academic paper and only the seminal work of French and Raven is cited. Many of the studies reviewed can be found in Bass, Bernard M. *Bass and Stogdill's Handbook of Leadership: Theory, Research, and Managerial Applications*, Third Edition. New York: The Free Press, 1990.

[2] French, J.R.P., and Raven, B. "The Bases of Social Power." In *Group Dynamics* (3rd ed.), edited by D. Cartwright and A. Zander. New York: Harper & Row, 1968.

[3] Bass, Bernard M. *Bass and Stogdill's Handbook of Leadership: Theory, Research, and Managerial Applications* (3rd ed.). New York: The Free Press, 1990.

Chapter 4

[1] For special insight, if you haven't yet, read Patrick O'Brien's books. Start with volume 1, *Master and Commander*, Philadelphia: Lippencott, 1969.

[2] A number of articles and books written about Japanese management and production systems present them as being largely egalitarian and familial in nature. Not only have some American companies established plants in Japan, but others have incorporated Japanese techniques into plants located in the United States, using largely U.S. workers. I will not discuss these models in detail here. I view the success attributed to these systems in Japan as being connected to postwar resurgence influenced by the halo effect and

a submissive culture. As many American companies have discovered, both uncertain economic factors and cultural differences make the adoption of these same techniques in the U.S. questionable, and today many are failing in Japan. Indeed, Japan itself has fallen on hard times and many Japanese corporations are abandoning their management models.

Index

About the Author

James L. Fisher is the most published writer on leadership and organization in higher education today. He has written scores of professional articles and has been published in *The New York Times, The Washington Times, Pittsburgh Post-Gazette, Palm Beach Post,* and *The Baltimore Sun.* One of his eight books, *The Board and the President,* "clearly established him as the nation's leading authority on the college presidency," wrote Michael Worth of George Washington University in CASE *Currents.* His *The Power of the Presidency,* was reviewed in *Change* magazine as "the most important book ever written on the college presidency" and was nominated for the non-fiction Pulitzer Prize. His most recent book, *Presidential Leadership: Making the Difference,* was reviewed as "a major, impressive, immensely instructive book...a virtual Dr. Spock for aspiring leaders, and...a must read for all board members.

A registered psychologist with a Ph.D. from Northwestern University, he is President Emeritus of the Council for Advancement and Support of Education (CASE) and President Emeritus of Towson University. He is presently a professor of leadership studies at The Union Institute and a consultant to boards and presidents. He has taught at Northwestern, Illinois State, Johns Hopkins, Harvard, and the University of Georgia and has been consultant to more than three hundred colleges, universities, and businesses.

Dr. Fisher has been a trustee of 11 private colleges and universities and two preparatory schools. A former Marine, he presently serves as a trustee of the Marine Military Academy, Drexel University, Florida Institute of Technology, and Millikin University. He has received awards for teaching, writing, citizenship, and leadership and has been awarded twelve honorary degrees. The faculty of Illinois State named their outstanding thesis award the James L. Fisher Thesis Award. The faculty at Towson University recommended that the new psychology building be named after Dr. Fisher, and the CASE Distinguished Service to Education Award bears his name.

As a university president, *The Baltimore Sun* wrote that he was a "master educational politician...under his leadership, enrollment doubled, quality went up and costs went down." In Washington, *Newsweek* magazine reported that, while President at CASE, his national campaign, the Action Committee for Higher Education (ACHE) resulted in "more than $1 billion in student financial aid."

For several years, Dr. Fisher did a popular daily radio commentary on WBAL, the NBC affiliate in Baltimore, and has been an occasional OP/ED feature writer for *The Baltimore Sun*.

Published Books:

Fisher, James L., and James V. Koch. *Presidential Leadership: Making a Difference.* Phoenix, AZ: American Council on Education and Oryx Press, June 1996.

Fisher, James L. *The Board and the President.* New York: Macmillan, 1991.

Fisher, James L., and Gary O. Quehl, eds. *The President and Fund Raising.* New York: Macmillan, 1989.

Fisher, James L., and Martha Tack, eds. *Leaders on Leadership: The College Presidency.* San Francisco: Jossey-Bass, 1988.

Fisher, James L., Martha Tack, and Karen J. Wheeler. *The Effective College President.* New York: American Council on Education and Macmillan, 1988.

Fisher, James L. *Power of the Presidency.* New York: American Council on Education and Macmillan, 1984.

Fisher, James L. ed. *Bibliographic Handbook on Institutional Management and Academics.* Washington, DC: National Institute of Education, 1981.

Fisher, James L. ed. *Presidential Leadership in Advancement Activities.* San Francisco: Jossey-Bass, 1980.

Other Books on Leadership
from Executive Excellence Publishing

Leadership from the Inside Out
Kevin Cashman

Discover a whole-person approach to leadership that reminds us that the ability to grow as a leader is based on the ability to grow as a person. The journey of self and leadership development focuses on seven major pathways to mastery in a multidimensional and interdisciplinary manner.
Paperback   **$15.95**

Moving Mountains
Reinhold Messner

What thoughts and feelings occupy us when we face our highest personal mountains? How can we be dedicated in pursuit of our goals, despite daunting hardships? This inspiring book is the best of best-selling author Reinhold Messner, the first person to reach the summit of Everest solo and without supplemental oxygen. Organized around his lessons on life and leadership, *Moving Mountains* outlines the secrets to overcoming failure, pushing the limits of the feasible, and achieving lasting success.
Hardcover   **$29.95**

The Spirit of Leadership
Robert J. Spitzer

This book probes deeply into all the major roots of organzational spirit, such as ethics, credibility, widom, fair conduct, charisma, self-examination, comtemplation, commitment, and purpose.
Hardcover   **$24.95**

Leadership for the Ages
David P. Hanna

The last two decades of transition in organizations have presented new challenges to leadership. Many leaders face mergers, downsizing, and acquisitions that threaten to destroy trust within their companies. *Leadership for the Ages* challenges leaders and commits them to a worthwhile vision of balance, demonstrating that the core of leadership is as timeless as the elements of nature. It is a road map as well as a "how to" manual for maintaining satisfaction with the bottom line while building trust. It represents the hope of leaders— the potential to achieve success, even in difficult times.
Hardcover   **$24.95**

To Order Call 1-800-300-3454 (toll-free)
or Visit www.eep.com